Instructions *from* Heaven

Volume 1

Awakening The Christ Within

Instructions From Heaven
Awakening the Christ Within
Volume 1

Originally published as
Instructions from Heaven for Living a Holy Christian Life, Volume 1

Original manuscript compiled and edited by Harold Dillard

Current edition designed and edited by Penny L. Kelly
Cover and Interior Book Design by Penny L. Kelly
Cover Photo – "Tranquility" by Andreas

All rights reserved © 2008 Center Space Media

Published by:
Center Space Media
32260 – 88th Avenue
Lawton, MI 49065
USA

ISBN 0-9820904-0-4

Instructions From Heaven, Volume 1/ Includes index
1. Spirituality   2. Prophecy   3. Religion   4. New Age

Dedication

This book is dedicated to the spirit and legacy of the man Jesus who became a fully Christed being while here on Earth and who went to great personal effort to teach and demonstrate what was possible for ordinary humans if they chose to develop the Christ-mind within themselves.

May His message be finally understood and the extraordinary truth about ourselves be revealed.

Table of Contents

Preface 7
To My Newsletter Audience 12
Prophecy Explained 13

All Who Can, Hear My Voice 27
Man's Honor 28

Instruction Given in Sunday Meeting 33
True Beauty 39
God Consciousness 40
Sunday Meeting Messages 41
I Am The Good Shepherd 45

Essence of Life and True Freedom 47

My White-Hot Fire of Deliverance 57
Superstition, Myth, and Fables 72

Fire of the Holy Spirit 75

Epistles of Revelation and Instruction 91
One Lord, One Chief, One Shepherd 101
What Man or Organization Can Stand Against Me? 102
Change Must Begin 102
Pray and Stay Alert 103

Resurrection Sunday Experience Results in New Birth 105

The Vineyard 123
Heights & Depths 124
My Fullness vs. Man's Good Try 126
Spiritual D.N.A. 126
Life, Truth, Emotion, Death 127
Blindness of Babylon 131
The Light upon the True and False Gospels 132
Peace with God 133
The Spirit of Jezebel 134

A Psalm of His Coming	135
Comfort My People	138
What is Growth?	139
Living Epistles	142
An Essay on Writing	145
I Need You	147
We Need Each Other	148
Know Contentment Anywhere	149
The Race to the Finish Line	151
The Oak and The Evergreen	153
Freedom From Despair	154
Flowers in My Garden of Joy	155
Hearing Lessons	156
The Jealous Shepherd	156
My Kingdom is Coming	157
To The Battle	158
Front Line Warriors	159
You Who Forget God	160
A Song of Battle	160
Horses and Chariots of Egypt	161
To C.W., By Faith, Not Sight	162
Tree of Knowledge, Tree of Life	163
Angels of Light	166
Be Born of My Spirit	169
Listen to the Voice of Your Almighty Deliverer	170
My Sword, My Famine, My Pestilence	172
See, Hear, Say, Do	173
Come To The Light	177
Exhortation to Purity	180
Purity and Perfection of Heart	183
A Prayer for Unity	184
Unrighteous Judgment	185
Vanity	186
Man vs. I Am	188
Mighty Harlot – Christendom	189
Tearing Down Strongholds	190

Forgiveness, Mercy & Love 192
Chosen Sons & Daughters 193
Heaven's Ambassadors 194
Surrender all 195
The Kingdom of Love 195
My Great Purpose 196
Wellspring of Life 198
Hand of Mercy or Justice? 198
My Peace 199
From Whence Springs Life? 200
Life Flows Forth 200
Power Upon Power 201
Street Kids 201
Let My River of Love Flow 201
My New Millennial 202

Man's Love vs. God's Love 203
Darkness In Your Midst 204
A Purging Cometh 205
Sure Current Words 206
One Mighty Shepherd 207
The Spirit of Jezebel Described 210

Glossary of Terms 213
Newsletters from Christ 230
Index 231

Preface

In April 2008 an elderly gentleman made an appointment to see me. He arrived at my home on the arranged date, came in carrying a white box, and sat down. Without preamble he held out the box and said, "I have been guided to bring you these books and ask you to publish them. Will you do so?"

After some conversation, I agreed to look at the books and call him with my decision. When he had gone, I looked though the books as promised and felt equally guided to say "yes."

As I understand it, the nine books in the set came about in an unusual way. Back in the mid-1990's a small group of people decided to get together each week to pray. I don't know what motivated them to do so, but the tone of the books suggests that they were disappointed with their church and the preaching or sermons they were being given.

They decided to get together on their own to see if God or the Holy Spirit would speak to them directly and teach them the truth, without it being filtered through the biases of any church.

It is not clear what happened in the early sessions, but by March 1996 they began receiving specific instructions to sit silently, without chatter or small talk, and wait until they either heard a voice speaking in their mind, or began to receive thought-impressions, then write down what came to them.

None of them were writers and some did not even speak English very well, however, they did the best they could and, surprisingly, a theme emerged in many of their meetings, with a number of people getting the same basic message, although it was always filtered through the individual perception of each one and written up by them in a uniquely personal way.

They gathered these messages and published them in a series of newsletters. Eventually they were put on the Web by Harold Dillard, and it was nearly a decade later that they came to the attention of Don Haughey, the man who brought them to me.

Don felt strongly that the message of Christ-consciousness contained in the nine volumes needed to be given to the public as quickly as possible.

When he first brought the books to me, the text was full of "thee" and "thou" and "shalt" and "wilt" and the messages were difficult to extract from the written words because of the twisted, archaic language used by the original writers. I told Don that, aside from the awkward writing, the messages in them were great. However, I didn't think anyone would read them because they were too difficult to understand. I offered to edit them into something readable, and Don said to go ahead.

As soon as I began to edit, I ran into warnings in the text that said not to change a single word or even a single comma. This gave me pause and I stopped in uncertainty. It was my turn to seek guidance and direction.

"Why did you bring these books to me to edit and publish if not a single word is to be changed?" I asked Spirit.

"Because you have a special way with words and you already understand the message. You *know* what these writers were trying to say. Keep the message but put it in your own words so a greater number of today's people will read them and understand," came the answer.

The Bible also contains warnings not to change a single word, so it is clear that the original Biblical writers were familiar with the shortcomings of translators, or of people who sought to change the meaning of something to fit political, economic, or their own purposes. However, both the Bible and these nine texts acknowledge that while the core message from God remains essentially unchanged over time, *the way it is taught to people must be updated to match the language, customs, and understanding of the people* from time to time. It must be kept current and alive.

Finally, I sat down at my computer, invited my good friend, Jesus, to sit beside me and let me know if I wrote anything that was unacceptable. We began to edit the work in such a way that the message would be preserved while making the messages infinitely easier to read and understand.

I have attempted to bring the message of these books into the present, preserving not only their valuable teachings, but the unique "voice" with which the original writers expressed the thoughts and ideas coming to them.

The group who received these teachings has disbanded and some of them have gone into hiding, wanting no recognition or publicity for their work in these nine volumes. Since some of the passages take Christianity and Catholicism to task rather brusquely, no doubt the original group also does not want to be harassed for speaking their truth so bluntly.

Regardless of whether you agree with their position on churches, the message of these nine books is clear. They state that:

… We all have the seed of Christ within us.

… We can develop this seed and bring it into full function just as Jesus did.

… Development begins by learning to sit still and silent long enough to hear the still, small voice of God within.

… This Voice speaks from the Essence of Life that runs through us.

… The answer we hear will come from the heart for that is where the Christ resides.

… Once we hear or understand the message or answer given to us, we must do as directed and to do otherwise is to "sin" or "go against the Life within the Self," which eventually results in death.

... Eventually everything we think, do, and say should be directed by the Christ within us.

... The development of the Christ in us is accompanied by gifts such as healing, seeing, intuitive knowing, visions, contact with beings from the higher worlds, etc.

... The biggest gift of all is the freedom from death and the ability to step into the state of being that maintains *eternal* life.

... The more we allow the Christ to guide and direct us, the more the physical body begins to transform into Light.

... As the transformation proceeds we will be forced to let go of the material world we have always known.

... Letting go of the material world is a pre-requisite for entry into the realms of higher worlds, also known as the "heaven worlds."

... The "second coming" of the Christ may be a group event triggered by a wave of grace that infuses those who have prepared.

... When this happens, there will be an obvious split in the world with any old systems that do not bring joy and peace plunging into chaos, while new systems designed to honor the Christ-spirit in man spring up to take their place.

If you would like to read the original text before my editing, it can be found on this website:

www.thehistoryoftheoriginofallthings.com

This book, or any of the other eight volumes, can be read straight through or used as a daybook in which the reader opens the book to any page and reads a single topic. Much encouragement for correct development of the Christ within you can be gained in this way.

It was a pleasure to work on these books, and the work allowed me to bring my own years of study and research into consciousness, plus my own experience with Christ-consciousness, in some small way to this work. It is my hope that if you have been seeking answers to your questions about God, Spirit, and the meaning of it all, you will come to understand what Jesus was trying to tell us…that *we are God* and must develop that potential.

Penny Kelly, Editor

To My Newsletter Audience:

To all of you who look for the recognition of man or the signature of man on this, My work, I say to you that I am Jesus the Christ, that the newsletter is Mine, the messages are Mine, the writers are Mine, and the ministry is Mine. Therefore, recognition is Mine alone.

Look to My Holy Spirit of Truth to confirm that these words do witness and testify of Me through these things.

Idolize no man within your hearts, otherwise you are still at fault and deemed to be in idolatry before Me.

Do not set your eye upon any man or ministry. Look upon Me alone, and walk according to My dictates. For the building in you of My solid foundations is My own work to do and will not happen through any man. You who have dedicated yourselves as My students will be built up in and by Me through My teachings to you contained in these messages and your own daily walk with Me.

Do not allow anyone to cause your downfall through your willing idolization of him. And do not cause anyone to fall by giving him glory that belongs only to Me.

From now on, know all simply as brothers and sisters, and no longer as living idols. Selah. For if you will allow Me, I shall build a new life in you and you will be overjoyed with the results of My work. Hence, yield your hearts fully to Me and let us go forth into purity.

Said by Jesus
September 11, 1996

Prophecy Explained

"It shall come to pass in the last days, that I will pour out My Spirit upon all flesh, and your sons and your daughters will prophesy..." (Acts 2:17), (Joel 2:29)

"Worship God, for the testimony of Jesus is the spirit of prophecy." (Rev 19:10)

"And this He is doing, has been doing and shall yet do in even greater measure as He is raising up both sons and daughters in this the end time. By the baptizing of them in His Holy Spirit they become able to operate various spiritual gifts. (Luke 3:16), (1 Corinthians 12:8), (1 Corinthians 14:5)

*T*he gift we will deal with now is *prophecy*. There is a great need for understanding by those who make up the Body of Christ on how to purify and perfect this gift, which is so necessary in this late hour, and to provide the help needed so that these children of God may become correct and pure in their prophecies, both spoken and written. So let us talk about this subject, with the Lord's help.

Hearing the Lord's voice is the first prerequisite to speaking or writing His[1] words. It is an awesome thing to be able to hear His voice to begin with, *never* to be taken lightly. This Voice is such that

---

[1] We will use He, His, and Him for simplicity and convention only. It could just as easily be She, Hers, and Her. The God within us can take the form of Divine Mother or Divine Father.

you *cannot* be filling your head with noise of any kind, music and preachers included, for *His is a still small voice*.[2]

He will not yell over the roar of what He terms *Zoe Babel*[3] or all the noises to which we are accustomed. He is the voice of our conscience, the voice of our deepest Self. He speaks to some by making them suddenly aware of signs in nature. He speaks to others only through impressions. And to some He creates impressions that our minds immediately form into words, so that we understand a complete phrase or sentence, writeable or speakable.

Those who are fortunate enough to hear writeable or speakable words should begin to realize that the prophetic gift may be operating in them. He is calling many to prophecy these days. Therefore it is the duty of each man or woman receiving this great privilege (i.e. His Voice in literal words) to begin not only heeding when He speaks, but also writing it down on paper and dating it!

There are many times He will give more, beyond the initial phrase or sentence, if the first things given are written down or spoken aloud, as in the case of praying over someone.

Our obedience is in speaking or writing that which was given, not knowing what will come next – either more words or simply silence.

It is a great gift when our Father makes His voice heard among the children of men. In truth, he speaks to many for their own benefit. Some will accept His message and speak or write these words from Him for the benefit of others.

When you write words and messages from the Father, it is important to put the date when these words were given because later

---

[2] See 1 Kings 19:12 for Elijah's experience in listening for God and finally hearing it in the sound of a quiet, gentle breeze. The message is that we must learn to listen over, under, and behind the roar of everyday life.

[3] *Zoe* means Life, and *Babel* means a confusing mix of loud talk, as with many voices, languages, or sounds being heard all at once.

you will want to study the message again. Since all of the Lord's messages are designed to teach you and bring you more deeply into an awareness of His presence and joy, each message becomes a lesson in the steps toward that end, and marking each with the date gives you a marker in time as to when He gave it and the steps to unfolding yourself in grace.

As with many old prophecies of the Bible which were written hundreds of years before their fulfillment, He also reveals the hidden aspects of reality and the fate of various groups. How good it is to know and understand that the Lord remembers His words and fulfills them, even over the span of generations!

Beloved Brothers and Sisters, He is raising up men and women[4] who will speak for him from the east to the west and is moving some of them to write and document His words so they can be spread among His people. Even though they normally do not even know each other, the message being given to all is the same, "Rethink your life and make new decisions about one another and how you will live.[5] Give gratitude to God who made the earth and the heavens, the oceans and the mountains, the trees and the flowers, and honor[6] Him by treating His creations with respect."

Thus, in obedience to Him, and despite whether you understand His message or not, write down and date the things given

---

[4] The original words used were *prophets* and *prophetesses* which literally means *"one who speaks for God."*

[5] The word used in the original text was *repent,* into which modern interpretation has infused shades of guilt, but what is actually meant by the word *repent* is what is stated above, "to *rethink* one's life and to *make new decisions about how you will live,"* in the hope that you will make choices that lead to life instead of death.

[6] The word *worship* was used in the original text, and in order to avoid the many religious implications of that word, which in today's world often implies mindless following, we have substituted the actual meaning of the word, which means "to honor and treat with respect or deference."

you and put these away for safekeeping until He shows you what to do with them.

The art of writing or speaking prophetically seems simple, but there are some important things about it that many do not know. First, let me say to all such speakers and writers that you should always pray that your Lord sharpens your hearing and perception of His Voice. Endeavor to free yourself from all outer and inner noise as much as possible, seeking to *practice His presence* and walk moment by moment in perpetual communion with Him in Spirit, actually talking to Him within and listening for His answers throughout your day.

You must not take this gift for granted! He has given you a talent of great importance. It is not just for your own benefit, but for the benefit of others as well *IF* you perfect that gift and do not hide it in the soil of your heart, keeping it to yourself.[7] You've been given a responsibility by Him. Do not ignore it. Rather, *nurture it* and *practice it daily* in back and forth dialogue with Him, as this will sharpen your perception and hearing of His words.

Now, man loves to sleep, but oftentimes He rouses a sleeping one to write prophecy. When this happens, rouse yourself and write with diligence, for the message coming to you is of great importance, else He would not have wakened you. Keep pad and pen close to your bedside and you will be ready to write if He calls to you. You may trick yourself into believing "Wow! I'll remember those words for the rest of my days," but you won't. In the morning they will be gone, so write them down, even if you are groggy. Many times, once the first line is successfully written, then comes a second line. When that is

---

[7] Matthew 24:14-30 talks about the problems of false Christs, chasing after earthly or human saviors, and the natural disasters that often accompany major changes in the world.

written, a third comes and so forth. You'll be glad you wrote the message, though your body hated the interruption of your sleep. Therefore, give heed to Spirit, and He will bless you. Your obedience in this is of great worth to Him.

And now I would give the instruction He gave me on writing or speaking pure words without "mixtures." There is much prophecy these days, yet often man's own ideas, concepts, and doctrines are mixed in it. For the beginner, these things are expected to happen, and thus prophecies are supposed to be evaluated.[8]

The method of writing without the addition of your own thoughts and ideas is simple, yet complex, requiring practice. Our minds are complicated – full of logic, reasoning, and storage of things. Minds function of their own accord without us having to work them voluntarily. We are always analyzing what our senses feed us of the information from the world around us. Then opinions are formed about what was analyzed. When we hear a word or phrase or sentence from God, immediately "our gears are turning," analyzing whether that came from God or us and what was said. It is at this critical beginning point that we must make a literal choice to either preserve or destroy the purity of the prophecy.

You must choose to write down what you heard and understood without destroying it by mixing in your own ideas and beliefs. "How do such mixtures come in?" you ask. They come through your own reasoning processes and analysis of the things being given during the time they are being spoken or before they are written down. Such reasoning would be ok if the word you are receiving is for yourself. But the word will not be *pure* unless you *hold back from all analysis* until He is finished speaking.

---

[8] 1 Corinthians 14:29 tells people to gather in small groups and if people are present with the gift of prophecy, channeling, or the ability to see signs and symbolism, they should speak *and* help interpret the meaning of what comes through so that everyone benefits and learns from the information.

Behold how good and how precious it is for brethren to dwell together in unity! It's like the precious ointment upon the head that ran down upon the beard of Aaron.[9]

This passage refers to an *anointing* – but what is this anointing? It is to receive spiritual gifts such as wisdom, visions, or divine guidance. [10] Aaron was being anointed for prophecy because of his ability to hear the voice within and share it in ways that would guide and help others.

We who hear and are able to write or speak the messages of the Lord are also anointed, thus it behooves each of us who hears Him to examine our gift and see if it is writeable and/or speakable. It is important to know and to practice this gift in order to perfect it.

We all know from experience that if you seated several people in a circle and one whispered a sentence to the one sitting next to him, and then that one whispered it to the next one and the message went around the circle, by the time it came back to the one who first spoke it, he'd find it drastically changed from what he had said. Why? Because of the reasoning of the mind of the hearer about what was said. Thus the meaning or the words, or both, became changed.

Of course, when we write anything, the mind races ahead as we write, thinking about what we are writing, deciding this and that, analyzing what we have said so far and what we plan to say next.

In prophecy, you must look at this in a totally different way. You must *turn off* this process of analysis and *not think or plan ahead.* Make an attempt to write or speak as right and pure as the Master intended. You must assume the role of the secretary who takes dictation from her boss. The letter he dictates is to be word for word,

---

[9] From Psalms 133:1-2

[10] See 1 Corinthians, Chapters 12 and 14, for more on anointing, which was often done during a symbolic ritual to acknowledge that someone had indeed developed Christ-consciousness and was a source of help, teaching, and healing for others.

and her opinions or thoughts about what is being spoken have no place in the message she is writing. Therefore, to combat this, she must clear her head of everything and seek to write what is actually being spoken.

The reasoning process is natural to us and goes on without effort from us. Thus it must be by exerted effort that we delay such powers of reasoning and analysis until the whole message is completed if we want to give the message purely as we received it. Now how important is it that we did not add to nor take away from the text? You will only come to know and thus understand as you learn through writing and seeing what tries to be added by your own thoughts. This is how text is marred, like LEAVEN being added to flour, that changes the whole texture and meaning so drastically from what was first given.

If you need to add a thought of your own or describe an accompanying impression or vision, clearly differentiate it from your prophetic quotes by parentheses, at least, or add it as a footnote. That way you can add something that figures prominently in the writing, yet not as if it were part of what He said

Punctuation is another great factor in writing and stating correctly. We can add our own zealous fire just by putting an exclamation point where a period should go and change the entire spirit of the message. The Lord has corrected me much on this very thing, showing me how, by doing so I have added fire to it, and that fire by no means aided His meaning but rather took away from it, and perhaps had a tendency to anger the souls who would be reading it. So in this manner, we must use much caution to get it just as the Master implies.

Shorthand is not appropriate in writing down messages from the Lord, for in writing shorthand, words are skipped which must then be added back to the composition later in order to fill in the blank places with logical additions. Oftentimes, we will not remember all that He spoke or how He used inflections and such. Thus, write it out in longhand as it comes to you and avoid losing or marring the purity and fullness of what was spoken. Don't worry, He will go slow enough to let you write it out. If you forget a piece, He will remind you so that you may go back and fix it to make it right. Be meticulous in attempting to get it just as He spoke it.

When He speaks THUNDEROUSLY or in other words LOUD, He means to use capital letters. He may change His loudness as emphasis in the middle of a sentence, so you must decide whether to use capitals on whole sentences or just one word or a few words, depending on how He speaks it. Do not worry. If He has chosen you as a writer, He will speak slowly enough for you to get it written down *if* you will be obedient in writing it. Don't be thinking about what He has said while you're speaking or writing it. Do not let your reasoning and analysis block the pure flow of His words. It's as He told me when I was learning: "First get it all down on paper. Once it is all written out and I am finished, you can study it, think on it, and analyze it all you want." Do not mar the purity of it while it is being written, do not engage in ordinary mental functions. In so doing you will inadvertently change the meaning, both adding to and taking away from the proper inflections while trying just to get it down.

Some attempt to postpone writing what they heard until later, thinking to remember it then. They might be busy at work, driving a car, or maybe they've nothing to write with or on at the moment.

In such cases it will be most difficult for what you heard to be saved in your memory in utmost purity. Therefore, because of your logic and reasoning working upon it, when you do write it, it will not be pure, but will contain the mixtures of your own mind's inflections, analysis, and determinations of what He *meant* instead of what He *said*. In this case it is best not to write such things in quotes, but to tell it in your own words as best you can remember it, using quotes only for words He spoke that you are absolutely sure were said. That way it will not be judged as wrong by those who hear it because it sounded more like you than Him. As you go on with your practice this will become obvious to you.

Now a *spoken prophecy* is different in that usually it is said to or for someone else to hear. Therefore, the spoken word that comes forth from you is *not to be remembered by you* unless it is being recorded in some way. In this way, you are not permitted to analyze it, except for the bits and pieces you are able to recall later.

As with written prophecy, the part of your mind which reasons and analyzes must be taken out of gear so your prophetic words can come forth in their purity to the ones for whom it is intended.

Heed my words in this – for with God it is a serious matter that you learn to use this gift in PURITY. It is not for you to add to nor to subtract from His message as you see fit. This is not yours to decide.

Today, there are many prophesying confused and incoherent messages because they have not understood, or they do not know or care that they mar the purity of a message by adding a word or changing a word or sentence. They do not understand how the message can change if you are being careless about punctuation and emphasis – all vital parts of a well constructed piece of writing of any kind!

You who are learning this – be aware! His prophets should all be receiving the same general message, though always the prophecy will show something of the personality of the writer or speaker. It is best to err on the side of caution and keep the words few but correct rather than the other way around in which you add your own thoughts and ideas.

Our God's words are very important and life-giving, and His words speak to each person a slightly different thing. Even though the message is similar, everyone will perceive it differently. It is a private matter between God and each person as to how they hear and react to the message. It is not your problem whether they receive the message – unless you ruined it with your own mind before they ever received it. In this, He will hold *you* responsible.

The gifts are given as a responsibility to us, His servants, to use for our own betterment and the betterment of our brothers and sisters. Consider it a *pure body ministry,* one in which it is your responsibility to perfect the gift you have been given. Do not hide your talent or keep it for only your benefit, which many are doing in selfishness.

The gift that is not used will eventually be removed and given to someone more grateful and ready to allow himself to be an instrument of his Master.[11] Prove yourself a worthy steward of this gift that He has given by practicing this dialogue with Him daily and be ready for writing when you go to prayer. Seek to hear and write His replies. You may be amazed to find He'll be much more talkative to you if He sees you are ready to practice and perfect this gift.

We who are given this privilege of prophecy must realize that we are chosen as messengers of the Most High, therefore our responsibility to Him is greater than those who received other gifts. As the watchman who calls to his brother to waken and to change his evil or slothful ways or suffer the consequences, you must give the messages to your fellow man or be held responsible for them. Apply the messages to yourself as well if you have been given the gift of prophecy and remember, the consequences of disobedience apply to you as well.[12]

---

[11] See Matthew 25:25-30 for the story of the man who entrusted his three servants with five talents each, and how upset the man was when he returned to find one of the servants had not done anything with his talents.

[12] Read Ezekiel 3:17-21 for the warning regarding the prophet who does not give his brothers the helpful messages he has received.

It is so sad to our Master that so many pray only when they want something from Him. They say a quick prayer and then get up and rush off, never waiting to hear His reply. If a friend wanted something from you and asked you for it, but then turned and walked away from you without caring to hear your reply concerning it, would it not hurt your feelings? In such a case, would you be willing to whole-heartedly supply it to them? Would you not shake your head and feel them to be a user of your goodness rather than a friend? So does the Father view those who do this to Him. For yes, He *does* have feelings; and yes, we *do* hurt them, almost continually.

This, Beloved, is a shame that we should be so blind and callous. When you learn to *be a friend* to Him, you will realize this childish behavior. All of us do this to Him at first.

So let us learn fellowship with him just for the joy of being with Him, and most importantly, listening for his reply. He has so much to share – a *wealth* of wisdom, of joy and love, if only we would be willing to wait awhile with Him, anxious to hear what He has to say. What blessings, what wisdom, what joy and love He would pour out on us!

I write these things to you, my Beloved Brothers and Sisters, by the commandment of our Lord Jesus, who is pouring His Spirit upon you.[13] He is raising up a mighty generation of prophets and prophetesses who desire to teach. Quickly their prophecies will come

---

[13] To "pour out His Spirit" literally means He is surrounding and enfolding each person with the energies of the Christ-mind in the hope that we will begin to attune ourselves to the high energy frequencies of this way of being and perceiving. As our brain-wave frequencies are raised to higher and higher levels, we will discover and develop the ability to perceive other dimensions of existence, known as "heaven worlds."

forth, so that He might pour forth His words to His people through them.

It is therefore *your* responsibility to perfect this gift by practice and diligence and to realize the seriousness of it and the consequences of ignoring it.

Shut off the noise in your mind so you might be useful to Him in this thing He has called you to do. We are a people used to noise, but He is one with a *still, small voice*, and therefore we must be quiet inside if we will hear Him. Keep in mind that preachers and preaching, as well as gospel music, have a contrary effect upon us in our growth, for by them we effectively deafen ourselves to His still small voice.[14]

You are in a most honored place if you have been chosen to prophesy, for you have the actual, literal Voice of your Inner Teacher/Comforter/Spirit of Truth to teach you by His or Her own voice. If this is the case, recognize that you have no need to be taught by man or his schools, for the Christ within will teach you everything you need to know.[15]

You have been given His Voice; therefore it is your responsibility to seek Him and to dine with Him at His own table, *learning from Him as He, Himself, wants to teach you.*

---

[14] Isaiah 30:15 tells us that the God we seek can only be found inside the self through remaining tranquil and trusting that there *is* a Self within us that is waiting to be recognized, developed, and allowed to come to the foreground instead of remaining hidden in the background of our lives. This God-self is called the *Christ within* and is developed by talking to it, trusting it, believing it is there, and responding to its direction and influence in our lives.

[15] See 1Letter of John 2:26-27; 1 Corinthians 14; and the Gospel of John 14: 26 for teachings that urge people to let go of what the world has taught you and instead embrace the power, knowledge, wisdom, and grace inside you, which comes from what is known simply as "the Christ within."

You are expected to at least try to stand on your own two feet, holding only His hand, for He is a very able Teacher, and you have a responsibility to let Him teach you.

Again, you have a responsibility to let Him teach you in His way, which does not agree with man's ways, traditions, concepts and beliefs. You are called to be separate and to be a priest or priestess for Him, even if it be a low one, because the testimony of Jesus is the spirit of prophecy.[16]

Therefore you stand as a leader already, not a layman. Take heed therefore, to this, and do not ignore the gift He puts within you. It is an awful thing to ignore or despise spiritual gifts, but *this one* could damage you worse than you know, for the message undelivered helps no one redeem themselves, so their blood will be on your hands! To whom much is given, much is required.[17]

The Love that flows from the Christ in us insists that we love one another, for each of us *is* love, and without this love we have nothing – no power, no peace, no wisdom, strength, or grace.

We are responsible for our brothers and sisters because, in fact, *we are one with them*. We *are* our brother's keeper. The beings who make up the Body of Christ are members of one another and of the wholeness of God. If the hand will not move to feed the mouth, we are in trouble. If the leg decides not to move the foot so it can step forward, we are in trouble. We must realize that we each have a part to play in this wholeness and cannot be just for ourselves, work just for our own benefit, or gather blessings for ourselves alone.

---

[16] The *spirit of prophecy* refers to interactions and communications that occur when someone has set aside their own thoughts, words, and ideas and allows the Christ within them to come forward and act or speak. The results are often different from what logic or reason might do, and they are often surprisingly accurate, effective, or miraculous.

[17] See the Gospel of Luke 12:48 for Jesus' teachings about how important it is to fully use the knowledge and gifts that we have been given.

Each has gifts for the edification and maturation of the Body as a whole and *not* as the churches have illustrated – a few showmen and a lot of lumps on a log – which is what we become in our pews under their teachings!

Be aware, my Brothers and Sisters, with this gift, much will be required from you. However, if you give your gift for the betterment of yourself, as well as the whole Body of mankind, what joy and happiness it will give you along with respect and wisdom! However, before I get you all out of balance, the Lord would remind you of what is also said about prophets...

A prophet is not without honor, except within his own house and within his own country.[18]♦

---

[18] This famous saying comes from Matthew 13:57

March 8, 1996

All Who Can, Hear My Voice

About Our Sunday Meetings

My question to you all is this: concerning your meetings, would you rather create a new sect or denomination, or do you want My Holy Spirit to reign supreme and to have the rule and liberty to do My work with you? You have your own form, so drop the form of religious meetings.

Pastors, cease teaching, so that all may come, seeking to feel only My Presence and to operate as My Holy Spirit impresses them. Let no one speak of the world outside of our meeting. All of you clear your minds so that My new impressions might be given. Seek to silence all thoughts so that you may be receptive to My input. Of course, all of you have thoughts of your own to share. This is "dialogue." Yet in order to hear that which I would speak, you must cease your "human dialog" and be silent within yourselves; so MY SPIRIT DIALOG will become evident.

If you want to be ruled in your meetings by Me, you must let Me have the floor. Do not try to say anything to fill the time, except – and *only* except – what I give you; and then, in respect for the others, return again to silence so that all may have a chance to receive and speak what I give them.

As My representatives, each of you, while in the meeting, has the power to build or to destroy. In other words, it is within the power of each person to respect the moving of My Spirit in the self and the other members and allow Me free reign. Or, you can dominate the time selfishly with small talk or your own ideas, wherein My time is lost and you are not aided. It is the responsibility of each of you to understand that silence and stillness is more beneficial and to allow all to have an opportunity to minister what I give them.

Therefore, meetings gathered in My Name are either dedicated to Me, or lost to whoever dominates them. If someone is always speaking or preaching, the service is not Mine, unless I am giving the sermon through that one.

Your meetings are to be a school of learning in how to operate the gifts I am bestowing. Therefore, many times, especially in the beginning, My Spirit is vexed and put out by your immaturity. Each of you – especially those who usually dominate the meeting – should be sensitive to others' desires to learn, and ALLOW ME TO DO MY OWN WORK.

Little Ones, this is *your* desire. However, at the meetings you often seek to get some things I must give you at home. This is one reason for your strong desire for Me – not enough time spent with Me. Still, in your meetings, I should have more freedom and leeway to move and minister as I wish among you all…and I will yet, if you let Me.

Thus, be diligent and LET MY WORK PROGRESS. Save all the small talk for after the meeting. While here, clear your minds so that I can do My work. This would be good, but are My people willing to do this?

Man's Honor

Men like statistics. They think this is a good way to measure their progress. However, you cannot judge your progress in this way. How many have been saved using statistics?

All credit for progress must be given to Me for it is My inner work in you that will be responsible for your eventual experience of salvation. If you think it came by one of your sermons, you seek credit for *yourself* and will boast about *your* statistics and in *your* church.

Even though you may put these statistics out in writing for all to see, then point them out and say, "Let's give the Lord a hand," it is not received by Me for I do not receive such honors from other men. Instead, it is *you*, in the process of pointing and declaring, who absorb all that type of honor.

All of you must consider where and how you receive – and like to receive – honor from men. Consider what effects this has upon you. What does it do to you inside? Does it bring puffing up rather than meekness?

Which one of you made yourself the way you are? None! Yet you take honors for the way you look or the way you dress. Those who have a lot of money to spend are preferred over they who do not have money. How is this fair to your brothers and sisters? All such boasting and receiving of adulations is hypocrisy, however, you consider it to be the mark of success, something well studied and coveted by men.

To all of you I say, CONSIDER MY EXAMPLE TO YOU OF MEEKNESS AND SOBRIETY. When I was here with you I did not act like the king or ruler of all, but as a humble man who surrendered Myself to My Father's will, even when this included dying to show you that you could learn to overcome death. I did not put on airs. My birth was not announced with fame and glory, with rich men attending, nor was it trumpeted far and wide. I was born in a stable amongst sheep and goats.

Beloveds, *be followers of my example.*

I did not seek to clothe Myself in luxury and ease, but instead sought to receive only the honor My Father gave Me. Thus do I please

My Father, for I am not a respecter of a man's person, his position, or his wealth.[19]

You would do well to be the same way, for all men are equal, despite their holdings or their looks. Did you not know this? No matter their color or their language, I have made all men of one blood, of one race, the *family of man*. Which of you, by prejudiced thoughts, can change this? It makes no sense to exalt one over another, or to set one below as if he were less than yourself.

In truth, if all men are given the advantage of higher learning, they can all advance equally, while he who thinks prejudiced thoughts is the lesser creature *because of his prejudice*.

O come and know the honor that My Father has given to all men – that of simply *being* the creature He made you to be. Honor one another as your fellowman, your *family* of man, and know that if you hurt your brother man you hurt yourself by this same action.

Consider yourself equal to one another. In My Kingdom the greatest is least and the least is greatest. How do you think? That the greatest is great? All who humbly seek the lowest seat will be given elevation by Me. He who seeks the highest seat will be given a lesser one.

Let every man examine himself or herself in truth and not be deceived. All of you, do not care for your appearance so much. Do not put on airs so that other men may honor you. The honor you receive is empty and worthless and puffs up your flesh, but does not edify or enlighten your spirit.

In fact, your spirit wars with your flesh over such matters and you are disquieted by these things. You do not realize you have been brought into bondage to the body and its ways, customs, designs, and habits.

---

[19] See the Gospel of John, Chapter 5, for Jesus' teachings on the importance of listening only for God's directions in our life and not giving in to the pressures and illusions of the world.

Beware of the world and its ways! Separation from it makes you no less a person. You will be no less "who you are" except in the eyes of those who judge everything wrongly.

Let My Truth shine upon your darkened judgment and bring all that to a quick crucifixion, for it is based on wrong thinking and I want you to understand this My way. Otherwise you will always be a slave to the thought that is in fashion and will respect only those who offer you some type of advantage because of their holdings or their looks. However, you will not be invited into heaven because you have these things. The invitation, issued only by the Father, is given because of *your attitude*.

So be aware – all of you – of how you treat your brother man and judge your sister woman. You hurt your brothers and sisters by thinking you are better than they because of looks or dress or wealth. Can't you see that this is putting on airs? This is the puffing up of flesh and strutting like the peacock, who is sure he is the greatest of all birds because of the tail feathers My Father gave him. He had nothing to do with making the tail feathers, but you cannot tell him this as he struts himself, nor can you convince those that look on and admire.

All of you will one day judge yourself using My criteria. What will you do on that day when you stand and look truly and deeply at what you have done? Your guilt will cause you great suffering and pain.

My Children, pay attention to how you *think*, and how you give attention or receive honors from others, for all selfish outward honor stains you. It does not help you. Rather it *hurts* you where I am concerned. Therefore let all such honor be laid in the dust from where it came.

Society judges you by looks, weight, clothing, position, holdings of property and wealth. But I do not judge by these things. I judge *by your heart and your attitude toward your God and your fellow man. Selah.*

Consider yourself carefully in the mirror of My Truth and let the light of It drive away the darkness of your thinking. In doing so, My Truth will break the chains that bind you, even those you are not aware of, and set you free. And if the Son or Daughter in you shall set you free, you will be free indeed. Free from what? The old mindset… the carnal mind and its thinking. You will walk in liberty and judge no man. You will be set free from all customs and habits that man has set up. You will be My Sons and Daughters and Servants, and no longer slaves to the ways of the world. You will be free to love all equally. Look to Me and changes will come. Offer up everything, asking for My help. I must help you and intend to do so for we are one in Spirit, and without the Spirit you are nothing.

Man can only teach what man understands. But he does not understand Spirit. I will teach all of you about this. Therefore be attentive to Me, all you who hear My Voice, that you may write it for the benefit of those who do hear yet. I will open your ears, if you ask Me, and show you the way into My Kingdom. According to your diligence, so be it.[20]♦

---

[20] See 1Timothy 6:3-11 and James 2:1-10 for teachings that warn against maintaining a variety of false standards in your mind to judge people, and about avoiding self-conceit.

March 10, 1996

Instruction Given in a Sunday Meeting

As you wait in silence, turn your mind gently away from whatever things come to your mind to distract you and return your attention again to Me. Multitudes of busy thoughts will certainly plague you from time to time. But you have control over your mind; your mind does not have control over you.

So take control over the wanderings of your imagination and slowly calm the myriad thoughts that come flooding in as you try to focus and center your mind on Me. In this way, you can take charge of the mind that seeks to wander aimlessly, even destructively, bringing it under your command. For you must learn to do this until it has become a habit to refer every thought, word and deed to Me.[21]

It always seems to be a difficult process at first. You will be tempted to quit because the mind is so active and unruly. But patience and diligence will pay off if you will keep up the effort.

You have the power to control your *self*, but part of you doesn't want you to know this. That part will make an attempt to save itself. You must overrule its desires and its power over your mind, for this is the way you will gain access to My way of SINGLE-MINDEDNESS, and we must become *one mind* if you want to reach the Christ in yourself.

Everything must be brought into balance. Even sleep, which many of you simply do not get enough of, will seem like a menace as

---

[21] In Philippians 2:5 St. Paul urges the people at Philippi to work at bringing their minds into complete oneness with Christ-consciousness.

you attempt to wait in the silence for Me. Do not be discouraged by this. Get proper rest and give Me time out of the BEST TIME YOU HAVE AVAILABLE, and not just before you go to bed, all worn out from the day. Wash your face with cold water before you pray. Do it again if you find you have been sleeping. Know also that the part of yourself that doesn't want you to succeed in becoming one with Me also uses fatigue to discourage you from waiting in the silence for Me.

I know what needs doing within you. Some of it you will *feel*, some of it you will *see*. I will show you things and we will discuss them. In this way we COMMUNE TOGETHER, as I did with Adam. Our communion will be sweet if you will apply yourself to the initial discipline, persevere through the troubles of staying open and silent, and fight the untimely sleep periods.

I SEE OVER AND THROUGH ALL THAT TO WHAT YOU WILL BE WHEN I AM FINISHED WITH MY WORK. Understand that I put great worth upon you, the creature that I have created. And each of you has magnificent potential for creation if you will open yourselves long enough and often enough for Me to do My work while allowing My hand to work through you for the purpose for which I created you. Therefore your diligence is required to put your ordinary self "to death" by insisting on solitude and silence within.[22]

What do you have in all the world as great and powerful as the *I Am?*[23] And to whom can you go for learning such as the *I Am* offers?

---

[22] Read Romans 7:14-25 for insight into the inner struggle that accompanies the decision to listen to the Voice within. Also check Malachi 3:1-3 for the message that warns that the Lord will enter suddenly, perhaps when you least expect it and will change everything about your life.

[23] The *I Am* is also known as the great *Void*, or the *Godhead*, the *Source*, the *Unnamable*, and other terms that try to capture in words something that cannot be described. It is a vast, eternal place filled with tiny dots of intelligent light. When you enter into this state of being, you lose all sense of

You are all in the same boat, being guided by the same carnal reasoning that brings forth death, as well as morality laws that are useless because they are imposed from outside you. If you look, you will see the absolutely imperative nature of My teachings for you – *just you.* It is My guidance that will bring you, just you, yourself, through each day of situations and circumstances, all having their own lessons to be learned.

See if you can find a speaker among you who can aptly teach you anything good. Without Me there is no *Life in your laws.* Until they are illuminated by My Spirit which manifests uniquely in each individual, the Holy Scriptures will be taught according to the letter of the law, according to worldly reasoning only. Because you have invited Me, I am here to show you that although you think you know a lot, you know nothing yet compared to what you *can* know – indeed WILL KNOW – if you will let Me be your Teacher.

So I say, as your Teacher: I come – not as men do, full of pride in their intellectual, worldly reasoning to teach you a thing or two so you may marvel at their knowledge – but AS ALMIGHTY TRUTH, THE LIGHT OF WHICH WILL PIERCE EVERY HEART AND ENLIGHTEN EVERY DARK THING WITHIN IT.

Can you endure this exposure to the Light of Truth? Prepare your hearts, for you will grow at the rate you can receive it, and you will know the Truth, who I am, and it will set you free. You will gawk and be amazed at the silliness and the blindness of your world even the way you, too, were before I delivered you.

---

self and become one with the Source. You *become* indescribable bliss and love, and you know immediately and without a shred of doubt that you are an eternal being made of this intelligent light. *If* something could be said to convey what you feel, know, and experience while in this state, it would amount to two words – *I Am* – and thus the ancients simply referred to it as the *I Am.* Afterwards, you are then said to have been *anointed* because you now know the essence of Oneness, which we refer to as *God.*

Come... do not be afraid. Let Me do My work in you, for this is wisdom and the simplicity of faith. I will not hurt you.

However, flesh that refuses to seek the light and insists on stumbling through the dark in order to have its own way will come to death. *You do not understand the laws that rule you without exception, and this is the root of every destructive, painful, evil, or sorrowful experience in your world.*

You pray to me saying, "Thy kingdom come..." But My kingdom must be built *in you first*. My will must be done *in you first*, for the *kingdom of heaven is within you*. Those who have found me within themselves pray constantly to Me saying, "Make me ever more conscious[24] of You, O Lord!"

My will *shall* be done in you, but not by the "free will" that men believe in, nor through your beliefs about your flesh. SPIRIT ALSO HAS A WILL, which I call "the will of My Father," and it is by allowing this will to express itself through you that you will finally come to Me and discover the peace, the joy, the abundance, and love that will fill you and teach you that you are without limit.

You do not know the work that I must do, but I will prepare you for it; therefore be diligent to come and open yourself to Me. Wait for me in the silence, watching and listening for what I will show you or tell you to do, then be obedient in all things and all ways

---

[24] The phrase in the original text says "You cry out asking ever more grace..." however, *grace* is the *awakening action* of consciousness that leads to eventual enlightenment and the understanding that the tiny units of light that comprise the *I Am* are intelligent and respond to your intent and the spirit of that intention. God is the *spirit of life,* and the will of God is the intent to *live.* Since we are one with God, every thought, idea, word or action projects an intention and form into the universe of being. That intention or form is aligned with either life or death and will eventually result in one of the other. This, in fact, is the *law you do not understand but that rules you without exception...* (from the paragraph at the top of the page.)

so you may learn and grow into full maturity as a Christ, which is what I am.[25]

How will you know if these are My words when they have been written by someone else? Ask yourself, "Who do they glorify? Some person? Or do they seek to edify every hearer and to clarify the glory of God?" In this way you will know the source of the authority; it will be either of man or of God.

Finally, believing – in fact, *knowing* – that I have heard your many prayer requests, listen carefully for My response, receive My instructions, and carry them out, for this is wisdom.

The anointing[26] you seek will flow when you learn to quiet yourself in Me. It is my business whether or not you need this anointing and it is not your concern; nor can you do anything to manufacture it or hasten the delivery of it. You will have it when it is necessary for you. MY GRACE IS SUFFICIENT, EVEN FOR YOU, My poor ignorant Children. I want you to let go of the state of ignorance you are caught in and move into that which is *spirit* and *life*. Come! Know that I am God and that I can be found in the stillness.

Christianity cannot stand the thought of this silence or that they must let go of what they think they know. They think they can help Me by their activity and their good planning. Beware! You will never find Me or enter into the heaven worlds using the ways and means of the world you have made

Instead, *just be as you are*. With humble heart and contrite spirit come to Me, knowing that you don't even know what to ask Me

---

[25] See Ephesians 4:13-16 for an explanation of how each of us develops in our own way and becomes an important part of the whole. This is often referred to as the "Body of Christ," and like a human body made up of skin, eyes, bones, blood, and the cells of billions of tissues, we are meant to work together to create a world that works as cooperatively as a human body.

[26] See Glossary of Terms, pg. 209.

for. Just know you need My help. This will be the most effective to approach Me and I will lead you according to My Wisdom and My will.

Moment by moment, hour by hour, day by day, walk with Me, holding me in your mind and heart. You have nothing to fear by following My Voice. You have a lot to fear by following men who congratulate themselves because of their great stature and wisdom among men.

Pay attention! When you come to the place where you know nothing as you used to know it, from that place I can work to reveal to you the heavenly wisdom that guides and delivers all to wisdom and safety.[27]

My people, what kind of gifts can you give Me? What can you do that will please Me? I tell you, *nothing* …nothing you can do will make *you* feel accepted by *Me*.

My Grace is within and all around you. *I Am the Grace* in every meaning. *I Am the Love* in every meaning. Immerse yourself in My Love and My Grace. I ask you to just *be* for Me. I need you even more than you think. My Grace is in you, so just relax in My Presence. Rest. Be Mine.

Be still and know that I am the Lord.[28] *Know* that the Kingdom of Heaven is within you. This is the way the Quakers started but it was so hard that they got into the fellowship of listening to one another instead of me, and thus were led to death.

Continue the practices learned here, and soon you will begin to notice the beauty and wonder of My quiet peace. Soon this short

---

[27] 1 Corinthians 8:1-6 reminds us that love is what builds the Christ consciousness within us, while earthly "knowledge" makes us feel self-important.

[28] The term *Lord* is an ancient title given to men who have achieved Christ consciousness. The term *Lady* is the title given to women who reach Christ consciousness.

time here will not be enough and you will want to continue the practice at home.

March 15, 1996

True Beauty

Clothes do not make a person. Faces do not make a person. Rather, look for the BEAUTY OF THE SOUL. It will either be obvious and most precious, or will be sadly lacking. Only by looking for the beauty of the soul will you see the true person.

You cannot like Me for My face or for My hair, and you cannot like Me for My clothes. You must see Me and accept Me as I am....a *Being alive in Spirit*.

You must also accept yourself without worrying about your face, your clothes, or your hair...and there is the real test. Can you accept yourself as you are, outside of the influence of these things?

Look at how the world thinks, and how they judge all things by what their eyes see. They do not behold the beauty of the soul. All they can see are their petty judgments, their competition, desires, and greed.

I say to you, let us see if the world accepts true beauty. Does it accept the beauty of the soul, which cannot be made gaudy with make-up, or covered over with clothing?

The truth is, I make a man or woman more precious than gold but this treasure is *inside* and all too often the world will not recognize or appreciate this beauty.

God Consciousness

Come into God consciousness and let go of the lower levels of consciousness for the lower levels of consciousness are earthly, based on the physical senses, devilish, selfish, and ignorant.[29] Judge no one by their body. See all men and women as equal whether they are tall and thin or short and fat, whether they are black or brown or white, have an ugly face or are beautiful to look at. Let these and other things make no difference to you for I have given each person a heart. Each is from Spirit and has a soul. By knowing and recognizing the beauty or ugliness of the *soul*, you will know the outcomes of each one's actions,[30] by which you can discern righteously between man and man.

I come to show you TRUTH. You cannot judge a heart by outward appearance nor by outward actions. None of you can discern correctly what is in a man's heart by outward looks or actions. But through Me and My Spirit you *can* discern, *via Spirit gifting*, what one is truly like. Notice I did not alienate Judas, though I always knew who he was, what he was sent to do, and even why. Yet I loved the man in his ignorance. I also dealt with Satan speaking through Peter, but thereafter I did not alienate Myself from him, nor love him any less.

To come into God Consciousness none of you can judge each other by past mistakes; nor should you alienate people and love them any less because of past mistakes. All of you err in judgment and action from time to time. I seek to bring each one of you to an equal

---

[29] Read the Letter of James 1:13-27 and 2:1-26 for an interesting lesson on mistakes we often make when we blame God for what happens in our lives, and for the importance of adding *action* to our thoughts and words. For without action, our beliefs and faith are useless.

[30] The words in the original text were "you shall know the fruit of every tree," which simply means that when you need to make a decision, you can know the outcome by looking at the inner intent of the man or woman with whom you are working and you will be able to determine the right decision.

footing in which all of you are accepted by each other. Then and only then will each of you be acceptable to Me. Therefore clear your hearts of all prejudice against one another, says your Master, Instructor and Guide.

March 17, 1996

Sunday Meeting Messages

The scars of pain are upon you, My people. Rather than responding to the pain, first offer these scars to Me and I will heal them, for these scars and wounds are always a problem to your peace and to your rest in Me. Therefore, with respect to Me, knowing I understand each heart and what this wound or scar is from, let each of you bring that problem to Me.

I embrace every one of you, My Children, in the great depth of My Love for you. You cannot know the bounds of My Love because it has no limits for you. I have the growth and benefit of every one of you in mind, and like the pretty flowers upon the table this morning, I would open you until you blossom fully. Many of you are still closed buds, full of excellent potential, yet not having enough of the warmth of My Love to make you open as have these flowers.

Be aware, each of you is a garden of the Lord, and each of you are My plantings, and I am proud of you. As I said, many are yet closed, but I bid you to feel and absorb My Light – My rays of *Son*shine upon you, and to blossom in that Light and warmth. I will operate through you if you will give me the time and the place to do so. Do not be afraid. You all are equal in My Sight and equally capable of blessing My other Children as I give you something to say, to write, or to do for them.

You are, each of you, depositories for the gifts of My Spirit. I come to fill each of you with these gifts. How can you say you are not worthy? *I decide this.* I, the Giver of gifts! Therefore open wide to receive My Love, for tremendous changes will come to and through you. My love and warmth will transform you – not today alone, but EVERY DAY. So walk, and open to Me. We will have this PERSONAL RELATIONSHIP, this LOVE AFFAIR in which you will be strengthened every day, and every day will be more excited to be with Me. You will be eager to take yourself forth in the world whether acceptance or rejection comes to you.

The world cannot touch your inner peace or disturb the rest of your Spirit as long as your eye is upon Me. Therefore focus, Children! I will cause you to shine as Lights – MY LIGHTS. I am the Light that shall first lighten the darkness of YOUR OWN PRIVATE WORLD. Then through you, My Light will give Light to all who are in the house. My radiant glory will burst forth and give Light to My needy world. Therefore, you lamps of the Lord, trim your wicks to Me. Be filled with My holy oil; be lit with the wholeness of Spirit and the Fire of My Love, and we will rejoice together.

Day after day I look at the sadness of your world with its suffering and degradation. Yet My joy is full. Why? Because *My* eye is always upon My Father. I work to fulfill His Eternal Will.

I do not look at the world in order to be caught up in its day-to-day happenings. Rather, I look BEYOND TODAY to the big picture, trusting in My Father, who knows all regarding the outcome of things. You, too, must be this way, My children, for if you look at the world and the happenings around you, certainly terror will seize you in the way it seizes those who have no hope. But I, your Lord and Savior, say *"Trust! And rest under the shadow of My wings."*

I, your Lord and Teacher, do My own work, and to you who are receptive to Me, I come to work through you. I will teach you how to use the gifts of Spirit, to teach My wisdom, use My power to heal, and use My knowledge to lead others to Me. It is for your sake and the sake of all that I come.

There is much work to do inside all of you. Therefore come to Me often and freely, not only here but in your homes. Do not be afraid to go where you can be alone and let us commune. Deep inside you already know how to *feel* Me. You may not all hear Me yet, but you know how to feel Me. *Open* to your deepest Self where I will teach you the operation of My gifts in order that you may be blessed and may also bless others. The more time you spend attached to Me, the more real the movement of My Holy Spirit within you will become.

Stay attuned to Me! I am Light and Life! All that men can hand you are dead, withered branches. I AM THE VINE OF ETERNAL LIFE. Remain attached to Me in your hearts, constantly receiving My Life and Nourishment. In doing so you will bear much fruit, and your fruit will remain alive and fresh.[31] This also fulfills My Father's will, for it is the will of My Father that you love Him and are successful in what He created you to do.

In the silence and the stillness you will find peace. Turmoil cannot enter in, pain and suffering fade, and death exists no more for My Life uplifts you! Death is the result only when you walk in the ways of the world, allowing your senses to entertain you. In the process of learning what *opens* you to Me, and what *closes* your heart to Me, you will see clearly what is Spirit and the will of God and what is flesh and the will of man.[32]

At first, every one of you will make mistakes at this, but do not be so afraid to speak for fear of making mistakes that you fail to speak at all. Remember, this is My School of Learning and you do not

---

[31] The mention of fruit here refers to the many successes and good results you will have, and the fact that they will continuously affect people in beneficial ways.

[32] The word *flesh* is used in the text, however, that word is too often thought to have mainly sexual connotations. The deeper meaning refers to the physical, mental and emotional uproar that results from participation in the world around us and which often creates such distracting dramas that we never discover the world of spirit.

yet know what you are to learn. You will know as I give you lessons. Open your hearts and I will teach all that is necessary for you. Let yourself want to be used so that you may minister gifts and blessings to your brothers and sisters, and in so doing grow in your own maturity.

Not all of you will hear My voice or see My visions and teach these to the world. Some will sing a song, utter a verse, or have a personal revelation, yet all will work to uplift the group and encourage humanity, and *none* of My flowers will be trampled underfoot, nor will I be trampled underfoot, as in some of your past meetings.

I know what is good for you, therefore trust Me, all of you, for as I said, you are all in the same boat, needing to learn the way of the Spirit. I rejoice in you being teachable regarding Me. Be flexible and able to change as I show you what you must do. This change will enhance you even as it puts the world to death in you.

I use My Word to heal you, but this will cut away your connections to this world that are in the way. Every one of you is being pruned by Me so that you will bring forth many good results and much fruit. Your fruit will be healing fruit, not the bitter fruit of man's reasoning or religion. Those fruits are bitter poison to My Spirit in you and they kill all, both good and bad. So let the sweet odor of your praise ascend to Me, even in the midst of My corrections. If you close because of embarrassment at My correction, let that be between you and Me.

I come as your Teacher, bringing Almighty Truth, and My Light will gently expose your dark places, bringing you to a place of understanding. Therefore prepare your hearts and cringe not. I come to glorify each of you and raise the level of your consciousness to create men and women who are wholly attuned to God consciousness. I do this because you have asked Me and because you are willing. Let no man or woman defend him- or herself when being corrected for this only makes matters worse. Come in humility, willing to give and receive forgiveness for your mistakes, for you are all learning.

I want you to eat from My table, each of you keeping in mind that this means My words are your Bread and My Spirit builds your Life. It is not the cracker or cheese that strengthens your body, nor the grape juice that delivers nutrition, or the fact that you come together to eat at all. Rather, it is important that when you eat – whether alone or together – you remain conscious of Me,[33] maintaining a high state of reverence and awe for the gifts I have given you.

Take time today to reflect on My words in silent contemplation. Have My words written down so they may be studied and shared with those who are not present for I love them as well. No one needs to dictate any of this during our time today. Rather each of you submit what you heard Me say by writing down what I brought forth in your heart this day. In truth, it is all between you and Me.

I Am the Good Shepherd

Have no fear; the Lord is here. But who believes our report? And to whom is the arm of the Lord revealed? It is revealed to those that are weaned from the milk drawn from the breasts of Christendom. The Truth of all the ages stands before you, knocking at your heart's door, waiting for you to open. Will you open the door to Me, your Lord and Savior?

Come, My children in need of learning. I have come to bring Peace and Life to your meetings and to rid you of the death that results when flesh reigns. Nevertheless, do not be afraid of this for transition must come. Instead, let Me teach you what you need to know, bringing you Life everlasting. Hope...trust...have faith in Me,

---

[33] The words used here were "do so *in remembrance of me*" which essentially asks us to remain aware of the fact that God is in all, and *is* all, even in the food we eat.

your Creator and TRUE PARENT. Will I give you a stone when you ask for an egg? Will I give you a serpent if you ask for bread? No!

The real serpent dwells in temples and churches and tells you that you cannot trust Me – your inner voice, the voice of your redemption. In spite of them, I have had some in every generation who walked and talked with Me and learned from Me. The churches *hated* them because they would not conform, but I love them; they are My own plantings and are not like the plantings of men.

Listen to Me, children for I am the Good Shepherd and am here to lead you safely to green pastures and still waters. You need not fear wolves for I, Myself, shall protect you.[34] Men will leave you uncertain and insecure and will flee to save themselves for a price. Therefore, listen only to Me, Children, and come to Me… *just Me*. ♦

---

[34] The 23rd Psalm and the Gospel of John, chapter 10, both encourage us to trust during dark days and to understand that the Christ is the good shepherd who leads us safely at all times and in all situations.

March 24, 1996

The Essence of Life
and
True Freedom

SUNDAY MEETING

#1 In the center of your being is something you can call *The Essence of Life.* It is on this *Essence* that you must learn to focus and upon whom you should depend. This *Essence* is part of the root of the TREE OF LIFE that runs through you, supplying you with Life-giving nutrients and sustenance, with wisdom and knowledge that does not come from the outside in but instead from the inside out.[35]

When you begin to walk this inner principle, when this *Essence of Life* is recognized, developed, and *lived* then you become a living Christ. When your Life, your words, thoughts, and deeds spring from the Truth contained in this *Essence,* then your old worries, fears, and efforts cease and My Rest enters in. It is then that the Christ Self lives and moves in you, and eternal existence is now yours.

Come, Children, to know and love and BE in Me. Know with certainty that I can be all things to you. I Am Life, wisdom, and happiness. I am a well of joy filled with everlasting, eternal Life. I am a Well within you and within all who come this way. I am filling you up with Everlasting Life. My Words are Living Water and are also your Bread. He who eats from Me will have eternal Life. He that eats

---

[35] See 1 John 2:24-27 in which he urges people to realize they have been anointed with *Life* and this "inner teacher" teaches from within, guiding you to eternal life.

from the bread of humanity's traditions, doctrines, and teachings will not have eternal Life and will continue to live in confused darkness.

#2   *I am the Lord, the Light, and Life.* I give to each of you a piece of My Life to share. And it is the responsibility of each of you to know when and how to share it. I counsel you in these meetings to pay no attention to what comes from outside and let this time of *spirit dialogue* replace your usual thoughts, ideas, and opinions. These are often harmless in themselves yet out of place here and therefore out of the flow of Life which I bring to your meetings. Hold your "small talk" and let this be shared at a later time. Instead be in My peace. I am moving in your midst to bring forth *fresh manna,* which cannot be stored overnight, and I want you to share in it.[36]

From within I come to each of you, therefore *go inside* to find the center of your being and the *Essence of Life,* for it is that which I want to bring to the foreground in you! Then you will be able to benefit the rest of the group.[37]

Let the things you do outside the meeting remain there for today is a day for fresh anointing and fresh words. My people have come seeking help; they have needs. So let Me minister Life to them through you. Do not stand in the way of this, rather rest in silence. Do not seek to fill the time of silence with words that I have not given you. Hold your attention on the silent place inside yourself where I live and speak, and I will give you *sure and current words* to speak for the benefit of all.

---

[36] See Hebrews 4:10-16 for both encouragement to persevere and admonishment that says "The word of God is something *alive* and *active*." Fresh manna is the timely and current knowing that guides us moment by moment. What happened yesterday and the guidance received then has no bearing on today. Yesterday's advice is like stale bread.

[37] Luke 17:21 reminds us that the "Kingdom" has to be created within us and then lived out by all of us together, thus creating a whole new world.

#3   Do you know the meaning of *freedom*, Children? Listen and I will give you the meaning. ***It means no death, but Life only.*** In Spirit there is true freedom from death because Spirit knows only Life. I am bringing you to deliverance from the life you think you have by yourself, to the Life that is available in Spirit. This Life is there for all who desire it and who will allow My hand to guide them. I *cleanse* and thus *renew* you. Those who come to me will be changed completely.

Christendom wants no part of My regenerative washing. They think that their ways of morality will suffice. They think that by following the rules of their religion they will be saved at last in the Kingdom of My Father. Yet I, Jesus, tell you that they are no more than white sepulchers; fair and holy to look at from the outside, but inside nothing more than a kingdom of flesh and selfishness! That is why I told the Pharisees to "make clean the *inside* of the cup and platter first. That way, the outside would be cleaned also.

Peter would not let me wash his feet until I finally told him "Peter, if I do not wash you, you have no part with Me."[38] My Children, consider My meaning when I say that if I, via My Holy Spirit, do not wash through you, you will have nothing in common with Me, nor I with you. Therefore consider the need for this inner cleansing. Your ordinary self is religious and willing to learn morality's ways.[39] But only if you let go of that self will you discover My type of freedom.[40] Be aware, that there are some who call

---

[38] See John 13:8 for Jesus' example of washing the apostles feet in order to demonstrate to them that it was necessary for them to give up their self-importance and to see that they must serve and take care of all people as equals.

[39] Proverbs 14:12 says "There is a way that some think right, but it leads in the end to death."

[40] In Galatians 5:13-18 St. Paul warns that "freedom is not an excuse for self-indulgence…"

themselves Christians but who are not. Ask yourself, are you doing this?

Know also that ahead of you lies great work to be done by Me through you. Consider that I have come to wash each one of you *daily* by the words I speak and by your own willingness to listen and act.[41]

#4   In keeping with the subject of freedom – MY KIND OF FREEDOM – what are you seeking here in this "land of liberty and freedom?" Is it to have yourself cleansed of the world and washed through by spirit, or to plaster religion over the garbage within while crying out, "Religious Freedom For All Men!"

Freedom from what? Are you free from deceit and lies? And what does this freedom bring forth? Does it bring forth *true* freedom? No! It brings forth more selfishness, more worldly pursuits, more greed and covetousness. Listen to Me, My Children, and believe Me when I say your world and your systems of Christendom are all turned upside down. Christendom is peddling fantasy and fables. Each of you can be My chosen, My elect, members of My True Church and awake to My Holy Spirit. *Learn the way of the Spirit* and not the ways of religious men. Those who embrace Christendom learn only the ways of the world, the lust of the flesh, the lust of the eye, and the lonely pride of the dark self. They are friends with the world and with those who no longer teach the way of My cross. They seek false comfort and want only to be at ease, thus they avoid the pain and work of entering the Spirit.

Beware! Hell fires are real for those who choose them! Death to the world of flesh *will* be experienced whether you do it willingly on this side or have it forced on you at your transition.[42] Decide in

---

[41] Revelation 21:7 reminds us that "water from the well of Life is free to those who are thirsty for it."

[42] The Gospel of Mark 9:42-48 goes so far as to suggest that we would be better off cutting off a hand or a foot, or taking out an eye than to let that

your hearts to bear your cross by changing your worldly habits now and let My Holy Spirit be the fire that burns out all your dross. In this way you can learn to raise your consciousness enough that you can dwell in the Kingdom of the Most High.[43]

The world is full of dogs, whores, obscenities, murderers, liars, and those that use their love to make a lie. Deception is for those that love it. Do not be a part of this! Wash away the idea that this is okay and attune yourself to my teachings. Only then will you truly be one with Me, My disciple and Friend. And remember, *sin, not self, is to be put upon your cross.*[44]

#5 Oh, little group do not think of your size, for it is the *I Am* that does the talking. You are communicators of My Word. Let Love radiate throughout the room. Do not force anything. Let *JOY* come to you. When your will *wants* My Will, the magic door opens to power for all things.

#6 Christendom has now been exposed. The opening of your eyes will deliver you from her illusion. She has mesmerized her subjects and put them to sleep concerning My Spirit and Ways. She has given them another way. But My Light and My teachings of Truth will show the way out of that trap and help you move into freedom.

---

hand be cruel to our fellows, allow that foot to walk the path of the unawakened, or tolerate an eye that sees anything other than love and compassion.

[43] In Mark 8:34 Mark asks what we have gained if we win the whole world but have not learned how to create a life in the world of Spirit. The answer is *nothing*, because worldly bodies die and buildings fall, while the Spirit body never dies and the heaven worlds are stable and eternal.

[44] Sin is any thought, word, or action that is not in alignment with the consciousness of the living God-Self that exists and breathes within each one of us. This is the true Self that we are being urged to go within and discover, then develop and live. It is this Self that is all-seeing, all-knowing, and all-powerful, as well as free from death.

My people are hungry and thirsty for something REAL, something TRUE, something that gets RESULTS. Nothing man has at present can deliver these. I AM THE SHEPHERD THAT WILL DELIVER. I AM THE ONE WHO CAN RAISE YOU UP FROM THE SLEEP OF DEATH. I AM THE VOICE CRYING IN THE WILDERNESS OF MEN'S HEARTS, SAYING, WAKE UP! WAKE UP! THE TIME FOR PREPARATION IS AT HAND.

The Spirit of the Lord does what He must, and if you do not keep up your practice of God consciousness, you will not know what to do or where to go and will be left behind. Therefore, Little Ones, as a hen gathers her chicks for a walk around the barnyard, keep up with Me. Do not hold not back, mesmerized by anything the world has to offer you. It is UNDER MY WINGS that you must be to be safe in the coming chaos. When it strikes, I cannot uncover you to go chasing after one, but must be stationary for the covering of those who are with Me at that time. Therefore, do not wander off lest you be consumed in that which will be.

Listen to My "clucking," the way chicks listen to the mother hen, and come and live very close to Me. For the end of things, the culmination of the end of the present Age is upon you. You do not know when it will strike *your* life. Christendom does not know either, nor can they find out, but they are all waiting and yet are unprepared. Can you see the danger in which they joyfully wait? Can you see their unpreparedness?

Little ones, be wise and know what My Will is. On the day when Judgment comes forth, whether you are ready or unready, you will know the truth of your own condition before Me. It is then that the judgment is set and the night comes in which no man can work any longer. It is then that the judgment and the bar come. Then My peace will be lifted from the earth – but not for My chicks, living under the shelter of My wings. Hear Me and heed My warning, all you who can, hear My Voice.

#7   Let every one of you be keenly aware of the needs of those who were not able to be here with you today. Do not judge or condemn them, for they all have their reasons and their right to them. Instead, offer everything to Me in Love and gladness of heart, rejoicing *for* those who could not be here, and asking that My Spirit do its own work, which you do not know, within their hearts and lives.

Remember, you are members with them of My Body, and we are members of the Body that is eternally linked together. When one part of My Body aches, all the rest of My members are affected. So pray for your brothers and sisters, knowing I Love them all and that I would like you to do this. Be glad for their lives for they are Mine also. Each of you has enough messages for yourself and others. Notice I give you Life by the barrelful, pouring Myself out upon you that you might have plenty to share with your friends, all My people, and My nation.

#8   Ask yourself from time to time how willing you are that I lead you? How much are you willing to learn? Open your hearts to Me, the Teacher of this group, and I will give you Life and Truth. I will expose the self that lives in the dark, and this will bring you to Life, leaving death behind.

Do not cringe, My people, but open your hearts to Him who knows all, sees all, and judges all in all fairness and equity. You are an example to all. Yes, everyone will know whether or not you are Mine.

I would make you a holy group with My Own Self moving among you, cleansing, purging, teaching, and giving revelations to each heart, each life, each soul. No man can do this kind of work yet, and each of you has specific needs you bring to Me each morning. Know that I am aware of them all. Offer them to Me and relax in My will. You *cannot* force me, and I *will not* force you. But My heart is drawn out in mercy to the contrite spirit and humbled heart. Therefore, know the way to come to the seat of mercy, for the way to My Ark is open to you. Do not come filled with the pride of religious information, for you will find the veil closed and the way blocked. Rather, *the heart of humility and contriteness of spirit* will obtain access to My Holy of Holies, the Ark of the Everlasting Covenant, for I Am the Lord who IS THE ARK.

#9 "There are six things that Yahweh hates, seven that his soul abhors: a haughty look, a lying tongue, hands that shed innocent blood, a heart that weaves wicked plots, feet that hurry to do evil, a false witness who lies with every breath, and a man who sows dissension among brothers."[45] Be aware of these and apply them to your own lives, each of you examining yourself in the Light of My Truth. For Truth does not come to kill you but to heal all the places where the world and your old nature has hurt you. I come to bring release from your prison and the captivity to those old ways. If you listen to Me when you examine yourself, I will pour out the Truth and you will see your need for inner cleansing. As Truth is revealed, offer Me your pain, your sorrow, your unwilling body/mind and behold, we shall have the victory.

At present, you walk contrary to Me and My Will in so many ways. You are so deeply based in human nature and reasoning rather than your God nature and your Father's will. Thus My training will be to guide your steps onto the path that follows My Way of Holiness.[46] This Way teaches you to pull your thoughts, words, and actions away from your worldly habits and begin practicing the Ways of the God

---

[45] From *The Jerusalem Bible,* Proverbs 6:16-19.

[46] The dictionary defines the word *holy* as "coming from God" and "deserving reverence." Since every single thing in all of creation comes from God, it is appropriate to think of *holy* as also meaning *wholly*, and "My Way of Holiness" can be said to be "My Way of Wholeness."

within.[47] Those that are diligent in their practice will become a shining Light, a mirror of Truth that reflects away all man's customs, plans, designs, and habits, illuminating what is Mine and Mine alone.

A thousand good sermons by the best known speakers from around the world will never deliver you from the mire of clay and the pit of SELF. Only by your own walk and talk, based in Love and the will of the Father will you reach Holiness and Purity.[48] Men's words cannot speak Life and encouragement to your spirit, but I AM THE LIVING WATER. DRINK DEEPLY OF ME AND COME TO KNOW ME AS I AM, FOR I AM A SPRING OF EVERLASTING LIFE, AND WILL BE SO IN YOU.

#10 You need a Teacher who will neither *add to* nor *subtract from* My Words of Truth, Life, Direction. All men seek Me in their own ways, but few have the ability to hear Me and write My Words for the benefit of all without adding their own opinions and beliefs. All who can – hear My Voice. All who can write it – DO SO.

Understand that many prophecies conflict and they should not. This is because many are hearing, writing, and adding to it from their own mind, or subtracting what they do not like of My Words.

You who are sons and daughters of men, I call you to be Sons and Daughters of God,[49] not by the will of man, nor by the teachings

---

[47] Titus 2:11-14 tells us that salvation is now possible for the whole human race if we will give up those things that do not lead to God, or *Life*.

[48] Purity occurs when we have cleansed ourselves of all fear, anger, vengeance, pain, sorrow, etc. What is left is love and peace of mind. When Jesus and scriptures encourage "purity," what they are really asking us to do is become aware of how many angry, destructive thoughts we generate, and then work to eliminate them, for these thoughts in turn create our world – which is a far cry from the world we all say we want. A "sin" is anything that creates a world we really do not want.

[49] St. Paul's letter to the Romans 8:14 says simply, "Everyone moved by the Spirit can become a Son of God."

of man, nor by the skills of man, but by letting Me lead you to My Father until you stand for Him in this world. I AM THE WAY THERE and now you are offered a way that does not lead *individually*, but *corporately*.[50] How will any of you know for certain where you are being led if you follow the world's will, teachings, and skills? I have a way of holiness that every man can find on his own, in which, even if he is a fool, he cannot err. My Way is that we walk together as Friends, that this walk be a JOY to you and not a grievance. Your own resistance, frustration, and fighting are the only things that cause it to be grievous. However, your willingness to let God's will be yours makes even the hardest part of the journey a JOY and a credit to Me.

My people, I lead you in the right direction. So listen to Me and the moving of My Spirit when I beckon you. Together we will make our journey to the high places[51] a success. The length, hardship, and monotony of the journey to these high places depends on you and your willingness to learn. So let us walk together as Friends for I Am the Everlasting Way-Shower that leads to the Father of all. Amen.◆

---

[50] *Corporately* refers to all of humanity, acting as one body, and just like in a physical body, each person plays a role in the wholeness of Life.

[51] The "high places" refers to the heaven worlds which are other dimensions of existence. These dimensions exist at much higher frequencies of consciousness and are populated by Beings who have learned to operate their consciousness over a much broader spectrum of frequencies. We often think of these beings as "gods" because of the abilities that accompany such development.

March 31, 1996

My White-Hot Fire of Deliverance... I Am the Light that Exposes the Darkness of the World

#1 The Master calls His chosen ones saying, "Rest in Me and let My peace overwhelm you. Let go of fear, even if My words in this newsletter frighten you. Yes, darkness does cover the earth and its people, but My Light will arise within you, and My radiance will be all around you on the day I bring forth the Christ in you."

You came and willingly gave yourselves to Me, putting your life in My mighty hand, so now rest and relax in Me. There is nothing that should consume your mind to the point that you cannot become quiet enough to receive My impressions this day. To the diligent I give all that I have. To the lazy and uncaring I can give nothing, even when I want and need to.

I am a nursemaid teaching Her charges. I am your root, your strength, and there is no power in heaven or earth that can deliver you from your difficulties except the power found in Me. So come and immerse yourself in My Spirit, letting Me nourish the gifts I have placed in you, bringing them forth for the benefit of everyone.

#2 You cannot force My writing, so just relax and rejoice. Rejoice, Children, rejoice! It will come. *I Am* is the Lord or Lady[52] within and it is your will that opens the door. God is pure goodness

---

[52] See Glossary of Terms for the meaning of *Lord* or *Lady*.

and love only, and it is the energy and power of this goodness and love that flows from Me and goes through you to bless, help, and bring joy to those around you. Don't worry about anything. *Love never fails. It is always present.* You will see signs and wonders when they are appropriate. You are My key group to encourage others worldwide to learn the power of sitting in silence and letting the Holy Spirit do all the leading.

#3 Why are you taken aback by My words in the newsletter? Don't you believe that I can make you as pure and powerful as I was while on Earth? Have you forgotten that it is Me within you that does the work? Do you think your body/mind is not worthy to hold or contain the presence of the *I Am*?

When you fully accept that you are a Son or Daughter of God,[53] you will no longer manifest your old self or any of man's unworthy characteristics. You will manifest My Light, Power, and Strength, My words of Wholeness, Purity, and Love, as well as My Truth, Decisions, and Judgments.

Therefore *you must empty yourself* of all your own curious opinions, thoughts, and prejudices. Empty out all your own private and inward judging of things and your ideas on how to fix them. These must all be released to Me for cleansing and purging of your old ways.

Search every part of yourself, enduring the Spirit of burning embarrassment and the shame that fans the fiery breath until My fire has burned up every shred of sorrow, pain, and guilt. Let it burn away all your great and marvelous ideas of how things *should* be, *would* be, *could* be, and all your plans for tomorrow, even your plans for today, coming just to *BE* and relaxing in God. Have no will or purpose for

---

[53] See Glossary of Terms for the full definition of a Son or Daughter of God.

anything except to allow Me to fill you with My holy purpose and will. Leave out everything of your own.

You are so full of yourselves and of your own or the world's wisdom that *I can do nothing with you.* You are quite sure you have all the answers. You do not know that you are *poor* and *blind* and *dumb* and *naked*, and without My assistance you can do nothing – not even breathe! Come, you proud ones, and tell Me how My creation ought to be changed. Tell Me, you haughty, of your plans for the future. I cannot use you so long as you will not empty all that proud garbage out of yourselves. Only the PURE IN HEART shall see God and know His will. The MEEK will inherit the earth because they are the only ones humble enough to listen and be guided correctly. The Kingdom will be given to those who will not steal it for themselves. It will be run by the HUMBLE IN HEART AND LOVING IN MIND, and there will be no one "in charge" but My Father. I, even I, Jesus, do not assume the right to run things, but in humility and submission to Him, take the lowest place.

Indeed, Man, you have a lot to learn of how little you know and how little you can do, especially in the time to come when all will be challenged, all shaken, while all the wood, hay, and stubble of man's ideas of greatness are burned to ashes.

Children of Mine, I require a cessation of all your planning, even of what *Sonship* is like. Give up, *as a sacrifice*, even the promise of a calling or of power from Me. Humble your heart and do not hope that you will be lifted up to a high position in Me. These are just proud thoughts. You high ones must become low, even in your own mind and heart, and humble yourselves to the dust, else you will not grow. Come to be equal with all. If your calling means too much to you, I will take it away to humble you. Do not lord it over anyone, for this is PRIDE AND ARROGANCE, a stench, and not the purity of the Sonship.

Hear Me, My people, even in this group. You are examples to the nation of what I am building, and I ask that you are not filled with pride by this, but further humbled at even the thought of it. I must begin somewhere to bring forth My holy work of manifestation from which Truth and Love will propagate and begin to manifest. If you are not ready because you cannot empty yourselves, then we must indeed wait longer for your preparation.

Let Me emphasize this to you all. All of you are nothing, regardless of the post to which I call you. Lying spirits will tell you that you are something special. If this happens, examine your habits and patterns, for who does not elevate himself, even within his own private self, because of knowledge or of calling?

Make yourself the servant of all and teach Love and humility. Most of all, teach *nothingness,* without which even I could not have been called "the Christ." Even being a Christ, I could say nothing from My own stores of reasoning and experience. I could not judge, even when judgment seemed obvious. I could do nothing from My own power. The miracles were all from My Father. I knew nothing on My own. Why? Because I emptied Myself of all My own ideas and aligned Myself with my Father. Therefore, you who seek to judge will be cast down in your pride and go back into My refining fires until everything has been purged from you!

And you, Little Ones, who endure My Fire, understand that this purifying exposure is good for you. The trials and tribulations that you find yourselves in also expose your own self to you. Can you see from these trials where you have failed miserably? They are for *your own* learning and growth, and *not* that of others.

Therefore, heed Me and *turn the judgment light inward on your self until your bad habits of mind and action have been burned out of you.* If you are haughty and full of pride, do not count on any glory. The credit you give yourself will be the only reward you get.

#4   Let Me be your example in all things. Humanly pride, even religious pride, will bury you. With pride, you will *not* survive My Fire. It will *not* get you into My Kingdom and will *never* win My approval. So many times you do not know the spirit of your own self. Can you see that you are wrongly judging others for whom I died also? You are quick to take the reins and say, "I will do this or that," when you can do nothing. You would be *dangerous* with My Power, and not only dangerous, but *destructive,* and thus I withhold it from you.[54]

You do not understand the inner laws that govern you. This inner law takes hold of your thoughts, including the judgments and condemnations with which you have judged your brothers and sisters, and *places them on your own head.* Thus you punish yourself using laws you know nothing about. This inward judging defiles and pollutes your energy system *and* is known and felt by others!

My law says if you judge others, the same judgment will be meted out to you. Thus, when you judge your brother, you *know not the log in your own eye. Clear it away first, and then you will see clearly how to help remove the splinter from your brother's eye.*

Only the proud and arrogant spirit judges another. Look at yourself and be humbled by how quick you are to attack and judge. Concentrate on your own weakness and failings and you will not be so quick to hate and judge your brothers and sisters. Point no finger at anyone, not even in your thoughts, for then I cannot use you and My Fire of cleansing only gets hotter. You become nothing more than ashes to Me.

Although My Fires blacken you, understand that, like the gold that blackens and runs as fire melts it, the blackness is your own dross

---

[54] In the Christ-state every tiny thought is extremely powerful and acts to create whatever the thought contains. Thus, if you have not let go of fear, anger, hate, worry, etc. *completely,* you would be extremely destructive to others because each thought or fear would be immediately carried out in reality.

and is burning away. Be aware that seeing your blackness instead of gold is a good sign that sin is being brought to the surface and melted away. The good you have is being kept and saved for My use.

Now all of you Little Ones, stop and take a breath in the midst of My Light of Exposure and see where your own failings are. You may cringe if you are honest with yourself. But know that My power cannot come and My Fires will not cease until you are purified of these inner habits of hate, judgment, and attack that disqualify you from My service. No one will be brought into Christ-consciousness until they have purged themselves of all arrogance and judgment and *the Spirit of their Life is pure Love and clear of all thought that does not come from Me.*

Surrender yourself to My judgment and do as I ask, for you cannot be prepared without it. Then, if you find you do not have My power, you will see the cause for the delay. By submitting yourself fully, My fire will burn away all the arrogance, competition, superiority resulting from knowledge, and desire to be honored and applauded by humanity.

Peter says, "If it is hard for a good man to be saved, what will happen to the wicked and to sinners?"[55]

Here you begin to see that the gate is too narrow for the big-headed, the pig-headed, and those who carry the baggage of the world. My Highway of Holiness is infused throughout with the bright glaring light of Exposure to Self, and those who maintain a worldly righteousness cannot bear to walk there.[56] Surrender yourself to be purged and refined so that you will be ready when the time comes.

---

[55] In 1 Peter 4:18, Peter writes that we should not let our love for one another grow insincere, and that *love will make up for many a sin.*

[56] See Isaiah 35:8 for a celebration of "the *Sacred Way.*"

#5　　Do not think how great the inventions of man are – the airplane, electronics, space walks, computers, and so forth. You are entering into *the creativity of God whose goal is to free man of himself.* How can this compare to the mere toys of man? Consider the caterpillar. Did he invent? No. He became, through death, the most beautiful creature, the butterfly, that spread his love to all.

#6　　My Little Ones, My desire is to cleanse you of your *self.* I want to burn away the desire to be "leaders" so that you may be "followers" of Me. Do you understand that My purified Saints will judge angels? How could you think you are worthy to judge anything if you cannot even rightly see and judge your own *selves*? You are incredibly stupid to judge your brothers. You do not know how deeply this wounds them, and *yourselves,* by it. Do you not understand that your brothers and sisters are a part of *you*? They are your own family! Or do you think you are better than they?

My foolish and ignorant children! Your thought-life must come under the rigors and discipline of My Law before you can die to your old ways of thinking and experience the results of following My Law. If you do not change your thinking, you will experience the results of those thoughts within yourselves.

Those who refuse to recognize and honor My laws, inner Light, and the Fire of cleansing will remain in the category of the lawless and will be judged as an actively destructive force. You can *claim* to have found the Christ, the Source of Life, within yourself, but if blessings come to Me from your tongue while curses go out to your brother man, then you have found nothing. A fountain cannot send forth both sweet water and bitter. Be aware that the bitterness fouls all of the sweet and makes it good for nothing.

Evidence of your *thought-life* is found in the words that come from your own mouth and you would be truly sorry if you could see the results. Therefore, I call you to be quick to hear and listen, yet

SLOW TO SPEAK. Do not give in to anger or rage, either outwardly or inwardly. Instead, be *forgiving*.

The *unforgiving heart will be unforgiven by Me*. Thus, if you want Me to forgive you, then forgive your brother man. Do it *seventy times seven* if need be, and pray for your enemies. Be good to those who use you, are spiteful, or abuse you, following My example. When you can do this, you will be the children of My Father. All men will know you are Mine if you have love for one another, are kind, and have a giving heart.

These things were the secrets of My doing. Put these things in your newsletter and know that My Cleansing Fire goes out through these words to purge and purify My Sons and Daughters and all who are ready to receive these words. This Fire will begin to birth them into My manifestation of Holy Power.

Do not strive for the place of esteem. Do not seek to be first or highest. And do not think you will escape My Fire, for no one shall lead that in any way prides themselves on anything that they *are* or *have*. Instead, acknowledge the High Priest of this altar, and sacrifice all of your own self and your desires upon it. Even Abraham had to give up the expectation that I would bless him. So must you, each one of you. Know that if I strip you, it is for your good. Therefore, hold fast onto nothing. Carry all things gently so that I do not need to remove it because of any idolatry in your heart.

You have called Me "The Potter" and you "the clay" in My hand. Do not be so hard within yourselves so that I must break you apart and start over. Be pliable and accept My Truth so that I can remake you according to My own specifications. This way you will grow into maturity by the fastest possible route. Your lack of acceptance makes your bed hard, and the fault is your own.

My Spirit is moving throughout the land, to bring as many as will receive Me into the Sonship. And *I will choose, not you.* Therefore, come to Me and open yourselves to My authority and My hand. That authority does not descend from any man or ministry, but from Me and ME ALONE. For I am with each of you as your Director and Teacher and as The Holy Spirit Comforter.

#7   Children of Israel, open yourself to My Cleansing Fire, the Fire which opens the door to My Kingdom of Love. Be ready to receive what I give you. Be ready to bear the fruits of this Fire, which burns only the evil.

#8   Knowing who you are in Christ is not vanity, it is reality. Do not let the material world dominate you. Spread your wings and fly; fly to freedom from worry of future or past. Reach out in faith. Love is a many splendored thing. Let it float out from you to change the world.

#9   Be of good cheer, My people! BE OF GOOD CHEER! Everyone of you are like teenagers who must be corrected in order to see things clearly. Every teenager sees things as if from within a tunnel. They have tunnel-vision. They cannot grasp the wider, bigger picture as long as they are centered solely in SELF and in their own opinion and experience.

You who have known some experiences of Christ and of God, open wider to full revelation and do not think you have it all. For the plains of Truth are infinite and boundless. Which one of you can claim to have all wisdom or all Truth? My whole Creation is a jigsaw puzzle! How many pieces of it do you see? How much of it do you truly understand? Trying to think about the whole of it confounds your mind. With such a thimbleful of knowledge and understanding, how do you think you could teach and instruct? Nay, none of you are ready or worthy Teachers, except you who submit your voice or pen or both to receive My Words for the people and say or write nothing but the PURE AND UNADULTERATED PROPHECY, MY SURE AND CURRENT WORDS!

Awaken! The Comforter has come, and He will reprove the world because of the sin and self-righteousness here. He will bring all to equity and balance, and He will restore the Truth that Christendom has stolen from you and eaten to fatten itself. He shall clean up and restore the old paths traveled by the sons of men who desired to follow Me, paths that were good and right and showed the proper way to travel.

I sent The Comforter to you at My Pentecost and gave Him to you as an Inner Teacher for all. But you have despised His leadership greatly and have chosen instead to honor man's wisdom, forms, and ways. As a result, He has left you to your own devices and thus you have experienced a falling away and time of gross darkness. You are now exposed to the Son of Perdition and the spirit of Anti-Christ. There is a feeling of desolation in your holy places, and you have let man teach you, lead you, and devour all good from you until you are not even good to yourself.

I do not speak foolishly. I am exposing GENERATIONS OF FALSE TEACHINGS AND FALSE FOUNDATIONS! I uncover them for you so you may flee from the Wrath that will come upon the devices of men.

My axe – My witness and testimony – will be laid to the root of the tree called Christendom, for it has been devised by men, and all its religious forms are man's invention. You cannot put Me into this – or any – bottle or mold for I will most certainly break free, destroying your mold in the process.

My sheep are hungry. They bleat miserably in their bondage and captivity to that which contains no life and cannot possibly deliver it to them. My way to deliverance has been blocked by hirelings and those who teach about Me for a profit.

Beware, My wrath waxes hot to deliver My little ones and I will not deliver them from one selfish and filthy teacher to another. So you who seek to teach or to deliver My people, first deliver yourself to My fire, and through My fire into absolute purity and perfection of Spirit. In other words, be emptied and cleansed of your *self* and all thoughts of superiority.

Come out of Christendom, all you Little Ones who seek Me by and through the teachings of men. The old house is crumbling, is about to fall, to make way for My Everlasting Temple, MY TRUE CHURCH, which has neither spot nor wrinkle. Deliver yourself from her danger, for My hand is falling upon it, and My cleansing Fires are starting within it, to *destroy man's ways*.

#10 The Kingdom of Christ-consciousness and the ability to step into it and manage your life from within it will be given to those of the highest consciousness, those you have traditionally called *saints*. They are called PURIFIED SAINTS because they have taken the time and energy to PURIFY THE SELF of old thoughts, attitudes, and behaviors.

And just what is *old self* and its sins or evil work? It is the part of you with the propensity to think that you are better, stronger, wiser, faster, or more adept at anything than your brother man with whom you are *equal*. It is the love of having an eminent job, or imposing house, or position of power with "all eyes on *you*" because of who *you* are. It is the way you puff up inwardly, like a great toad, because of the admiration of others. It is sloppiness in any form, rudeness to anyone for any reason, or carelessness to one who is hurting. It is insensitivity to the needs, thoughts and feelings of others. It is greed and covetousness and clinging to worldly supplies and things, especially after I have told you not to worry about such things. It is the holding back of help and assistance to those you see in need, for whatever reason. It is the filling of your mind with the thoughts of your own importance and how you should do this or that, when your brothers and sisters need you to purify yourself and let yourself be prepared to bring deliverance to them. It is allowing yourself to be blinded by your captivity to Christendom.

Sing all the songs of deliverance you want but until your own interior becomes My Kingdom, and My will is done therein, then you are lost and your good works are nothing. You may as well leave your brothers and sisters to their own fate, thinking "poor stupid people, how can you be so dumb!"

The vision you have of how to help others will not come to you through your own intelligence but will be given to you *by My decision* so you can help your brothers and sisters.

Your responsibility now is to let Me cleanse you, purge you, purify you FOR THEIR SAKES. You who say "My walk and my progress are mine to delay, and I can take all the time I need for I can only save myself," be aware of how selfish you are in your heart. To whom much is given, much is required! You who look upon My poor and blind captives, grieved by their blindness and stupidity, and do nothing are no different than they. Do you think I endowed you with sight for your own self only? To those whom it has been given to hear the plain words I speak – why have you not shared them with the rest of My people? Why?

The world you see around you *is* the harvest field given to you, My Sons and Daughters, to gather! Therefore, all of you who claim to be Sons and all who wish to be called Daughters by Me, *see the harvest fields! Are they not white with harvest?* So why stand there, idle all day? Apply yourself in your preparation, for you are by no means ready. Be diligent and serious and quit thinking you're just waiting for the other poor slobs to get done with their preparation! Pride does not make you ready, and when a man thinks within himself that he is ready, that he has attained the Christ-mind, it is then that he is indeed *not ready*. He is only ready to fall. Beware, you that *think* you stand, lest you fall. And let those of you who know your calling *offer it back to Me upon My altar,* for I must give it back to you before it can truly be considered "yours."

#11   To *will* and to *do* is within your power, either to use for yourself or to give to Me. Surely this is unknown and unpracticed, mostly because I cannot enter into any heart that does not invite Me, nor can I be "Lord" over any life not captivated by Love for Me. How can I be Lord in a heart filled with selfishness, a place where *I, me,* and *mine* rule supreme. Many call to Me in this hour, saying "Lord… Lord…" yet cannot hear what I say to them. They think they can attain the Kingdom by works of their own design or to influence Me using words with no true meaning.

Foolish, foolish man! Your religiousness will obtain nothing for you. *It is the real, heart-felt prayer I receive. And the true repentance that is complete I receive.* What can you give to Me from the forms in your religion except the fruits of the world and works of darkness? In all your focus on religious ways you have forgotten that these are the works of man, and that men are idols and not Gods. You do not know how to "save" any man, including yourself. Remember, this is the reason you first came to Me.

WORSHIP GOD ONLY AND ABOVE ALL ELSE, NOT ONE ANOTHER! And how would you decide who to worship? Comparing is not wise. Children, return to your Maker, your Savior, your Deliverer. Turn to the Christ within, your First Love, and do once again the work you were first created to do. I see all humanity clinging to religion's purpose, pursuing religion's way, and soon to be consumed by religion's death.

FIND ME WITHIN YOURSELVES and come away from your idols of men! For only that which is given in the silence and stillness of your own heart will endure My Fire. That Fire is already in you, burning you, incinerating all of humanity's old desires you once held. Submit to My cleansing Fire and call the next newsletter

My White-Hot Fire of Deliverance. I AM the Light That Exposes The World.

#12   Come to me, all you who are wrapped in chains of your own making, for fear is the lock and Love is the key to open your prison doors. If you are going to fear, *fear Me*. But truly, I ask you to revere Me, to hear and obey Me. Only fear My judgments if you insist on willful disobedience. My cleansing Fire is not to be feared but rather understood, for your preparation for perfection is necessary yet is not taught among you.

This preparation is so necessary that if I were to remove it, every one of you would die in your sins, a castaway. Therefore, praise Me for My fire, which burns away your dross and exposes your *self* right in front of your face so that you may see yourself as you are and be humbled by it.

The teachings of men only lift up the proud heart. "Yes! We will reach the Kingdom by force and obtain it for the Lord by our superior strength and wisdom and numbers and votes!"

O People! IGNORE THAT NONSENSE! Can you hear that this is merely Self boasting, gloating, and exulting itself? Everywhere, those of religion say, "We shall overcome!" But they will overcome nothing by such claims, and will deliver no one, not even themselves. Those who seek to obtain the Kingdom by man's device, man's wisdom and reason, man's numbers and force will see no light and will dwell in darkness and in dryness, inhabiting the parched places of the wilderness. Even though denominational hands join in unity with other denominational hands, they will all fall together. I see all and know all and by religion shall no man SEE ME or KNOW ME or WIN ME.

#13   Unless I wash away your old life, you will have no part of Life with Me. Remember this as you take My Bread – Your Life –

and as you drink of My Spirit – your Life Cordial. Believe this within the depths of your being. I am come to claim you for My own, all of you, even that which Satan has tried to steal through allurements common to each of you. Your heart is a territory to be conquered and won. Your life will be a sweet sacrifice to Me.

Your whole life is to be a sacrifice upon My Altar and the giving of yourself over to the Father's will, dominion, and cleansing. This includes your thought-life, heart, and mind. Therefore, bring *all* out of captivity to the world and deliver yourself to the dominion of Christ. Have this in mind as you silently and singularly taste of My Table.

#14 Self-examination is so necessary that without its continual practice and processes you would all deceive yourself. Thus practice it continually. Let it yield the fruits of humility and meekness with a self-effacing mind and heart. Then you can embrace your brother and sister with purity, freedom, and love. Your embrace must cease to be "show" and become real and true. In this way each of you will cease to hide behind your masks of fear, harboring your own secret sins of thought and feeling that you hope others will never see.

Offering these things to My Cleansing Fires is the most important thing you can do. Otherwise, your life will never be without fear, your conscience never at rest, and your mind never stillness and peace. Only when you have dropped your old habits of mind and heart will you know the peace and purity that is possible for you. As long as you have thoughts and feelings you hide, things *not* offered up to the Fire of cleansing, you will suffer. This is what the discomfort of My Fire is for – *to force you to stop thinking and feeling the way that you think and feel* while believing you have hidden these offenses from yourself and your brothers and sisters.

Until your own complete obedience is fulfilled I cannot use you to deliver others or to do anything. See the greatness of the task and move with haste to complete the circumcision of your heart to Me. Cut away the foreskin of flesh you are hiding behind then CONTEMPLATE AND CONSECRATE your whole life to Me and to My service. Leave your Life or death to be My decision. Let go of Sonship or Servanthood and let this be My decision. Make no effort toward glory, or persecution and rejection, but instead know that ALL of your life, whatever I decide it to be, will be a glory and a praise to Me alone, which will be praise enough for you. Purity – the complete absence of destructive thought and action – and knowing the right use of everything I have given you in this world will make you like new creatures.

Superstition, Myth, and Fables

The red man is a curious being for he holds on to one thing while reaching for another. Therefore he is subject to superstition, myth and fable, which was his downfall the day I tried to instruct him to save his life. In the same way, My Christian peoples are also curiously subject to superstition, myth, and fables, adhering so tightly to it that they loathe the onset of the new for fear of losing the loved other. This will be *their* downfall as well, for holding onto superstition, myth, and fable will result in these, in turn, falling upon him and drowning him in sorrow and doubt.

The myths and fables of religious attendance, of servitude of women to their husbands, of tithing, of assembling by force, or of impressing a man or place or thing with "authority" were all added to the book. The idea that men should have short hair and women only to have long hair was also added. The separation of church and state was added by changing words to denote this, thus CREATING MYTHS AND FABLES AND SUPERSTITION in the minds of men and women.

Nevertheless, My Truth lives down through the ages undaunted in its quest to deliver My Creation from itself. It will seek to bring forth Light, Inspiration, and Revelation through the willing hearts and receptive pens that allow Me their time so that I may give it forth. Therefore all who are willing, seek to make yourself ready for and worthy of My dictation.

    Given by your Master, Jesus. ◆

April 7, 1996

The Fire of the Holy Spirit Rests Upon the Heads of Those Who Seek to Be Led by Me

RESURRECTION SUNDAY
EASTER, 1996

#1   The *fullness* of My Revelation to the Apostles was not given at or before My Death, or even at My Resurrection, but at My Pentecost when the Holy Spirit was sent forth to empower, reveal, and enlighten the hearts and minds of all who waited for the appearance of My power. All who tarried there received My Holy Spirit and with it revelation and enlightenment. However, not all received the fullness of power that My Apostles did, because all could not understand its use at that time. Nevertheless, all began to utilize Spirit's gifts.

    Look for My Revelation to come, as well as the manifestation of My Holy Power. Do not be in a hurry to leave or watching the clock and putting limits upon My time with you. Be flexible and not rigid for today is most special, most holy to Me because of My Resurrection, and not because of My ignominious death at the hands of wicked men. So stay and wait, and be imbued with power from on high, a *gift* I give to you, along with Myself and the Resurrection of Life in you!

#2   Knowledge is like a safe haven, and in study there seems to be much wisdom and learning. Adults like knowledge and take pride

in it as well as shelter under its wings. But there is *another* form of knowledge, that of a *child*, who knows nothing, reads nothing, yet is filled with joy at the environment in which I have placed him. Does he cease to learn and grow? No! For he is always learning new and curious things. My point is this: Unless you become once more like a little child filled with the wonder of the *I Am*, you cannot see or enter My Eternal Kingdom.

Man will never learn to know God through earthly studies. All his studying is of no use to him unless he does it *in* God, with God opening and showing him the eternal and spiritual meaning of what he learns. When man remains in ignorance he feels he must DO something or READ something – yet from this he only becomes more confused. Why? Because when he sought to teach himself, he left out his Divine Teacher and chose man as a teacher. The two are *incompatible!* The Lord must let you choose who you want as a teacher. So understand that it won't be Him *and* others. No man can serve two masters nor can he think he is serving and loving one while serving and loving the other.

Thus, hear the law of the eternal kingdom. Whatever reading you propose to do, let your will be totally open to Me first and seek My approval. Only after I give it should you read – and do so carefully. If you sense no Life in the words and there is only "head knowledge," lay the book aside. The husks of men, though good to the eye and ear, rob the soul of the nourishment I give you. Be faithful to Me and listen when I tell you to lay aside everything which I do not approve for you.

The child does not cease to teach itself, however, it remains in innocent wonder until words are put in front of it. Then it explores this new realm, where reason and doubt and opinions are formed. Soon the child learns to be prejudiced and stingy, becomes unruly and stubborn. Those who have learned to be this way cannot enter Christ-mind at this stage of growth, but must unlearn what they have learned from men, and this includes what they have learned about Me and My

Kingdom. Open yourself only to Me and My inner cleansing and teaching. This way I will teach you My foundation truths, which have not yet been revealed to any man...so stay open to learning and receiving from Me.

#3   May the blessings of the Lord or Lady, your God within, and your Risen Lord Jesus, be upon all of you. Be at peace, you children of an immortal race. Though in the flesh you close your eyes to sleep the sleep of death, yet your soul and spirit take their immortal flight in Me.

Your beauty is like that of a newborn child to Me. Let your faces be turned upward toward the Light which I pour down upon you, and let yourself be enlightened by it evermore. I AM THE RESURRECTION AND THE LIFE. You can come to Me. So let it be. I give Myself to whomever will follow Me into the depths of My inner cleansing that washes away the old ways of death.

Rejoice in Me and the newness of life. Take flight in Me, your *sky,* and live a Winged Life. Fly to the heights and soar and wheel about in greatest joy, and find that with the same ease that you have flown to the deepest depths you can now enjoy the highest heights. Keep your mind on My Freedom and know that I, your Deliverance into the realms of Spirit and Freedom, have come to take you with Me. Come! Know My Resurrection within yourselves and let the deadness of what has passed be past. Let Life and Joy be yours.

#4   This is the day the Lord has ordained from the beginning to the end to the new beginning. In the end days the Lord, Himself, will resurrect a Remnant to complete Himself here in the earth Kingdom. The fullness of His Promise, the completeness of His Truth, and the blessing of His Remnant will be a sign of this end days reign. As the world tried to subvert, distort, or diminish His former works, now shall He do likewise to the works of men, first in mercy to the elect, and later in judgment to those who reject His gift of grace.

Let he that has an ear to hear and he that has an eye to see, hear and see that God does not speak in vain. It will not be as mankind has envisioned but by a more divine intervention than man can or would prescribe. There will be tearing and rending of all you have held dear for millennia. A new, complete, and incorruptible foundation will be laid down, and within all who hear the cry to come up hither He will build a new Life.

#5 I will build up a new House fashioned from those the world has culled and cast away. My House will be based on all that man has disdained. It will be simple and not ornate so that humanity will compare their standards to Mine and be ashamed at their ostentation. I find the simple, the humble abode, to be of great price and greatest value.

I will overturn the thoughts and delights of men until all see the stench of their riches. Riches will be like a millstone around the necks of the inhabitants of the churches and cathedrals. Everyone will see and know My intent, and pastors will be dismayed when I say to them, "So *THIS* is what you have done with the money for My poor! Depart from Me all you who do not love your brothers – the brothers you see every day. Depart from Me all you who hoard treasures yet tell the hungry, "We will pray for you, now go away. Soon you will be full." I will say to those men as they sit and banquet in excess, "Go away and be *full of what*???"

In *one day* I will take it all away from those unfaithful stewards. If only you would allow Me to bless your "two fishes and five loaves," *multitudes* could be fed and I would bless all with My abundance. But if you do not seek Me then I cannot bless you... and that is not by My design or intent! I say it *should not* be so, and in fact, it *will not* be so. For I, this day, will take away all that you have and your plight will be worse than your brother, whom you chose to ignore. The choice is yours. Hold tight to what you have and lose it by My hand or release it to My purpose and plan. You choose, and do it this hour: Will you be blessed or cursed by Me?

From now on the Kingdoms of this world are the Kingdoms of God, the Creator, and are given to His Son, your Redeemer, *with or without* governmental consent or debate. Choose to delay or ignore My words and you risk the punishment of My anger. You are not dealing with another neighbor nation but with God Himself. He will deal with you individually and will reward or set up whom He wishes and will cast down whom He wants. From now on you will see His hand at work, all you inhabitants of the Earth.

#6   All will be shaken until not one stone will be upon stone, for the old will be cast away and not remembered again. Truth will be the currency by which everyone and everything will be measured. Anything not established in truth will be destroyed. Come to My spiritual bank and make a withdrawal, for only I can give you any good thing. All that you have and all that you have known bring only torment, despair, and death to your soul. Do not allow your flesh to cripple you as My Kingdom is established. Release everything to Me that I may be all-important in you. If I am not first within you, then your tomorrow will be damnation, I promise you. However, if you have opened and filled yourself with Me, then your tomorrow will be a blessing for you and all you touch and meet.

I deal now with individuals. All who thirst and are hungry, come to Me. Eat and be filled with that which lasts eternally, without money or fearing what you should wear. All who come will be received.

#7   Give yourself to the Light and resign yourselves to the dictation of the Spirit. You can hear nothing so long as you seek to

DO anything. So relax and clear your mind of all that you think worthy, whether of scripture or of song, and know that if it is coming from Me you cannot put it off because it will return again and again, bidding you to write it. If it does not come to you again three times, it was not of Me and was not Divine Guidance.

As you write, the messages need not be numbered until the end. Once all the messages have been gathered together, they can be numbered sequentially. However, keep them in the order received, which is necessary for the proper flow of My instruction. It is up to Me to see that the messages flow together from various individuals. Your responsibility is simply to listen, to receive, and to write it. Be aware, My Nation waits hungrily to receive it. Not your words, but Mine. All else is the shadow of death and great darkness.

Therefore on My Resurrection Day – which is what you *should* call it instead of "Easter" – *BE My Light* of Holy Inspiration and let My Life flow without competition from other thoughts, ideas, and spirits. Lay aside all your own opinions, wills, dreams, and aspirations, and let My pure message come forth. Amen.

#8   I speak comfortably to you, My Spiritual Israel. Your captivity is over, your death pardoned, the price paid. I have stamped out the bill of your divorce from the world, all you who lean wholly upon Me for your learning. I make My Covenant of Life with you forever.[57]

Rejoice and sing at the turning of your captivity for *you are My True Church, born of the New Jerusalem Mother*.[58] The sweetness of your inner, humble praise is like incense that is witnessed here and

---

[57] See Hebrews 8:8-13 for an example of the Lord's willingness to forgive.

[58] See the 1679 Prophecy, given by Charles Price, in which full redemption would be made possible by the birth of a new church that had no connections to any existing churches.

testified by Me. So let us walk together as One, writing the messages that will deliver Creation, My Nation.

I have other sheep who could not be with us today. To them I speak. I wish to gather them to Me and My teachings, wherever they may be, so that I might RESTORE to them the Life that Satan has taken away through various religious manifestations to which they have become accustomed. I do not seek to congratulate on you this day. Rather, I will cause you to write My Words of Life to those who are still captives, those who yet choose death by sacrificing their greater good through ignorance and tradition.

My Love for them is great, and I want them to deliver themselves out of the lands of their captivity! On this, My Resurrection Day of rejoicing, I feel a hint of sadness and a twinge of remorse for these Sheep who are still lost from Me. They wander in the dry and barren pastures of Christendom, feeding on the bark of twigs and dry cactus, thinking they receive nourishment, when I, the Fountain of Living Waters and the True and Immortal Bread of Life stand by, wanting to give them LIFE and REAL FOOD for their soul.

So let Me pass this Bread and Water of Life through you to them. Let this be a time of intense watching to receive the bread I give, which is to be sent to them, for all our rejoicing will be hollow noise without the others whom I am calling and seeking to deliver. Thus rest and relax. Listen deeply and hear. Write and receive My Words of Life for them that they might be delivered *into* My Kingdom and *out of* the kingdom of Christendom, the kingdom invented by men.

Listen and hear, mankind. My speaking is not yet turned away from you and My hand of mercy is stretched out still. The *grace* of your Lord Jesus Christ is with you and is sufficient for you. My strength comes forth in response to your surrender.

#9   A new Life is dawning for you today, new Life Everlasting. Rejoice, for today I begin a NEW and GLORIOUS thing, a COMFORTING, DELIVERING thing, which all the world will marvel at, but not all will accept. I bring you My Pentecost.[59] My power and anointing now falls upon your heads. I have called and ordained you to help all of mankind.

You are right to rejoice along your own path, but seek to see the *bigger* picture, the plan and purpose of Creation. You have been chosen to be the Hands that deliver My Love to My Creation. Understand that *together we must bind the strong man* who holds My poor sheep captive. Only I know where he is and how to deal with him, so if you will let go of your own opinions of who he is and resign yourself to My *full* leadership, it will be done. I know, My Sons and Daughters, that you have ideas aplenty, every one of you, of who the enemy is and how to subdue him. But under the guidance of ONE, who is your Captain and Commander in Chief, we shall work in unison with one another; and it will *NOT* be every man for himself, or any and every strategy used that can be imagined. Only in unity do forces succeed, even in *your* wars. So let Me be King of the battle and we will carry out My war only as I show you. With Me as your Immortal Commander, we will have good success.

#10   Christ-consciousness is the name of the game. Don't sleep your way through life. Knowing Christ deeper and deeper will come as your will trusts in Him. Let this Easter Day be a day of rejoicing that inspires all.

#11   Halleluiah! Forget the world and its troubles. Rejoice that you can hear Jesus talk to you and guide you moment by moment. Do not

---

[59] *Pentecost* means *fiftieth*, and the term became special because the twelve apostles became filled with Christ-consciousness 50 days after Jesus' death and resurrection. They had spent that entire 50 days praying, meditating, and fasting.

think that this is old stuff. If you want something new, open your doors wider, open your soul wider. The *I Am* is never dry, never empty.

#12 Why dream about the past? That's gone forever. Salute Jesus for the miracles He has wrought. Why worry about the future, the *I Am* is here, now, with you forever. Join the adventure in faith and there will be no boredom and none of the world's cares. Enjoy your new freedom and thank your Father for it.

#13 I am calling you to a higher consciousness, My Children. I am calling you up and out of the lower thoughts you have been used to. I seek to lead you into a higher Life and a more spiritual existence. Your future is in My hands. Believe that I seek this higher life for you and it will be yours. It is My will that My children go on to reach perfection[60] just as I have.

#14 I am a God of mercy. I do not hold your mistakes against you. I want to deliver you out of your unhappy ways, O My Creation. But I need your help. I need your cooperation. Come to Me and I will show you the way. It is not difficult. Only believe and it will be opened to you. Amen.

#15 I am a God of Life and Spirit. I seek to lead you upward to the worlds where My Eternal Light shines, a vision of which you do not have now. Wait quietly for Me and you will be given a higher vision than you have now. It is My will that you seek this higher

---

[60] *Perfection* is reached when not one angry, worried, fearful, vengeful, unloving, or destructive thought is generated to mar the deep inner peace, joy, and love that flow from you naturally. The result is entry into Christ-consciousness with its all-seeing, all-knowing oneness. When you can remain in this state regardless of what is happening around you, then you are *pure* and ready for life in the heaven worlds.

Light. It will be yours, but you must wait quietly for Me. Ask and it will be yours. Calmness is *faith* in action. I will come to you as you remain calm in Me.

#16 I am merciful and kind to all who come to Me. I will forgive your sins and pardon your iniquities. I will remember them no more. Look to Me and save yourself from the world you have created, My Children. I truly seek to deliver you out of the *abyss* of your own making. I am leading and guiding you to higher ground. Do not be discouraged. Do not be afraid. I love you and will walk with you until you have been delivered from this world.

#17 Greatness, mercy, and love flow to all today in this meeting dedicated to Me and My Name. Resurrection to real Life entertains you as I come bearing gifts of Life eternal and the *heat* of My Spiritual Presence. I, your Lord, am happy at the plan and purpose of My Father to use you, Precious Ones, to help deliver My Creation. Open wide to receive. Fling open the doors of your heart so that the KING OF GLORY may come in.

Arise and shine, for My Light is in you and My glory is rising within you.[61] Let yourself wonder at the path I have chosen for you, and be constantly amazed at My handiwork. Long have I watched you, My Beloveds through times of tears and sadness, then times of joy and exhilaration. Your times of sorrow and sadness were allowed by the wisdom of an All-Wise Creator, who thus forced you to change, to adjust and correct your ways. These things happened without your knowledge so that you might be more useful to Him.

The rough file of impatience coming from others smoothes and refines you immensely while shaping you carefully for My service. You think My corrections are so rough that you can hardly

---

[61] Read Isaiah 60 for an amazing description of the promise of the Father to any group or nation that develops and lives in Christ-consciousness.

bear it. Yet I know what is rough, calloused, and hardened. I know what must be removed so that you may be softened in love towards your brothers and sisters. I know that you must learn *to love and forgive them in spite of anything they do,* as they, too, are growing.

Move in haste to display the Love of your God-Self. Be simple and undemanding in all things, for if you are rigid, you must be broken until only pliability remains.

O man! O woman! The world of My Kingdom must not be forced to conform to you; you must force yourself to conform to it. So become soft and pliable by My healing streams of water. I fall as dew drops on all My hardened clods that they may be softened and readied for My planting.

#18   O foolish men! Who has bewitched you and forced you to drink bitter gospels? Why seek men to teach you of Me? You even seek men who know less of Me than you do!

Have your riches convinced you to retain the hireling to tickle your ears and soften your conscience? Where is their power? Did they heal anyone today? No! They cannot even heal themselves. So why do you seek an empty wisdom? Is it for advantage to your business? If so, I suggest you go to a trade show gathering. Your houses are *desolate* for I cannot be found there. Even those I send to give My Words to you are censored and cast away. My days of dealing in your tombs of the dead are done. Come away from them and come to Me that I might fill you with My Power, My Promise, and raise your consciousness until you step into Eternal Life.

#19   Do not think in the same manner as men, and I will show you a mystery. *I Am* in everyone according to the accessibility of the individual. I do not discriminate against anyone and receive all who come to Me. I bless each according to the measure of their openness.

Some come close and I give them much. Some come only part way, so can only receive part.

Too often, men regard some people as heathen savages, but all races are My own. Anyone who harms My Little Ones will suffer the same punishment themselves. Historically, punishment has been sent to individuals, families, and even nations on behalf of perhaps only one of My Little Ones whom I deemed to be wronged unjustly. Humanity does not know which ones are Mine, but *I do*, and I am a Protector of My Little Ones.

I will do many things in My coming Reign. Seek Me in all things. Treat all with love and patience and do not rush to judgment of anything while you are still subject to such faulty decision-making. If you falter, I will take matters into My hands, something not to be taken lightly.[62]

#20 Know, Children, or more accurately My "shepherds," when you feel you have something to prove, I cannot use you and your desire toward Me is tainted by self-will. Surely the enemy will use this to dig at your brothers and sisters.

Therefore, it is most important that you surrender your wills as well as yourselves to My holy dictation. Lay aside all your reasons, excuses, or purposes in honor of that which I will unselfishly bring forth, even if it is My Holy Sword to cut away flesh. See My Plan to deliver man from himself. The plan is to deliver My Sheep.

---

[62] Hebrews 10:26-31 points out that the laws of men change. The Law of Moses was replaced by the New Law taught by Christ. This passage in scripture says, "We are all aware of who it was that said, *Vengeance is mine; I will repay!* When Jesus says things like "My punishment," "My wrath," or "My judgment," he is speaking as one who has totally aligned himself with God and is so completely identified with God's Law that He can say things like "*My* judgment" because, in a way, it *is* His. The difference between Jesus and the rest of us is that He remains humble and aware that God does it all, while we get uppity and stray from that alignment, bringing judgment down upon ourselves.

Only the rebellious shepherds who have taken advantage of others will come to shame and condemnation – all by their own hand. They have taken advantage of the poor and have been cruel to My Sheep, imprisoning them through bondage of the mind.

#21 The demanding ways of the world's religions judge things in error, pride, and arrogance. So it is My Way and My Law that hands out the same judgment to them, which indeed will occur. It will be a *just* Judgment, reflecting the blindness of their own minds and the hardness of their own hearts.

Yet to the simple, My laymen and laywomen, and those who do not throw their weight around but remain open to Me, I will come with comforting words. They will be words of warning that push them to free their souls from that house of bondage, the house of Ishmael. I will call them to My New Jerusalem Church, or else My destroying Sons will have no choice but to serve My destruction to them as well.

Through My Sons and Daughters I will come and surround Christendom with words of wrath. They will be like the walls of a fortress surrounding her on all sides. Therefore she cannot escape, lie her way out, or deliver herself or her followers, but will fall completely and be destroyed – swept out of the way for the coming of My Kingdom and a Millennium of My Reign.

So watch and wonder at My doings. Seek to become fluent at hearing and writing My Voice, for the published words will go forth far and wide as a testimony against all that is false. Martin Luther is proud of this that I now do, which he *tried* to do but could not. The time for such things had not arrived yet. Amen.

#22 The spirits of those who served Me in past ages now stand with you to encourage you in every way to follow the path of

deliverance from your low lives.[63] Though they *saw* it in their day, they could not bring it forth for their fellows. Deliverance was not given to that age by My Father, but to *this* age, in which the end of the current world will come.

This is so intensely important that I cannot leave it in the hands of man to accomplish by his ideas, but must directly communicate with every seasoned soul I employ. *You need to become fluent in hearing.* I will surround all who come willingly and contrite, all who seek to be used honestly and humbly, with My Spirit energy.

As you begin to *see*, you must lay aside your prior knowledge – seen as through a glass darkly – and begin to develop yourself until you reach My state of perfection. This state, available *in* and *through Me,* is referred to as SONSHIP, which is a realm not only of salvation of yourself, but of others, for then you become MY BREAD to hand out to others.

Do not seek to fill yourself only. And Handmaidens, do not hide My words anymore! Bring forth the words I am giving you by having small meetings with *no form or advanced personality in charge.* Dedicate all the time to My Holy Spirit, thereby giving up all your own ideas, works, and energies to be prompted by The Father, your Comforter. I will be with you every meeting and promise I will teach and speak through you, using what I call "prophecy" until everyone present has been brought out of the world and delivered.

I warn you and all who are attempting to exit Christendom. Do not hold to *ANY* form nor count anyone outside yourself as your Teacher. Otherwise you still hang onto a form or structure you think will save you. You must divorce from *all* your old ways, former

---

[63] A *low life* refers to the condition we live in when we get in the habit of allowing our consciousness to remain closed, sluggish, and caught in the back-and-forth rules and traditions of the world. Awareness remains minimal, fear is ever-present, and our experiences of the possibilities that are open to us in the world are limited. Thus we never rise to the higher forms of consciousness and life that are possible.

works, and even their songs and worship service formats to win Me, your Teacher and Guide.

Be like little children, again – *all* of you – if you want to learn the way of the Spirit. In this way, the move that I make across the land will widen and spread. There will be nothing that you can do about My Fire breaking out, and you can by no means put it out. The Fire that revives and renews all will sweep through your nation, and no man can take the credit for its beginning. No heart need lift itself up in pride to say, "I caused that." It is simply the time for Me to reign and once again possess all that is Mine.

Christendom is doomed. I pronounce it in her ears. Purity in all its fullness is coming forth, a grand and glorious gathering of those who have become Hosts on High.

#23 Love's sweetest sound is *obedience*. Love's grandest chord is *praise*. Love's greatest sacrifice is ALL that one *has* and *is* to the service of the loved one. So inhabit the realms of the Kingdom of Love in the splendor of all you *are* or *have* or *ever could be*, laying yourself down for your lost brothers and sisters, even as I laid Mine down for you. All who live in the heaven worlds as Christs in Jesus see themselves as equal, meek and quiet of heart, holding others as better than they, all seeking the lowest place.

#24 I pour the equivalent of *volumes* through you to My People. *Volumes* have been lost by the will of evil men in their efforts to control others. Thus much has been left unspoken or branded unlawful for the ears of men. But My power to draw others to Truth is great, and I will get more and more intense for the time of awakening is now at hand.

Expand your newsletters to incorporate all My new and indwelling words to the People, and do not fail to publish them quickly. I want all men to see Me coming, first to the joy and gladness within themselves, or at least to the fires of shame and disgrace as they begin to awaken and see themselves truly. I AM THE WORDS OF LIFE, THE WORDS OF ALMIGHTY GOD. So if you have seen and heard me, listen carefully, for the time is at hand for the end of all things made by man

#25   Number the messages according to My dictation when they go into the newsletter format. Do not number them now individually, but do put them into order for copying and make enough copies for all who are not present. Send or take copies to them so that everyone in the group has received My words and can grow.

Before you do this, take of My Supper quietly, reverently, and individually because my teachings are between you and Me alone. Come therefore, Children of Mine, eat from My Table and receive copies of the messages I have given through each of you, messages that confirm My words through the pens of two or three witnesses. And then, depart in peace and acknowledgment of Me, for I love you, I hear each of you, and I acknowledge you. ◆

April 1996

Epistles of Revelation and Instruction

#1 If a man follows God while remaining perfectly open to discover his purpose in life, he will come to know that purpose through revelation. By no means can a career path chosen by man sustain him, nor can he come to the knowledge of God's reason for creating him except through revelation.

Thus, no man is Christ's own until he has the seed or voice of Christ operating in him, nor can he be called a S*on of God* until he has been a *student of Jesus, the Christ*. The voice or spirit of prophecy working through him will lead him and guide him to that perfect purpose his Creator intended on the day that He created him.

All souls are unaware of God's plan for them until it is revealed by revelation, and nothing can be revealed so long as man holds to his own reason and power to decide what is "good" or "evil," "right" or "wrong." Because of his perverted judgment he cannot even begin to understand these things, and through disbelief and rebellion he rejects that which is true. He ends up holding onto a lie which is half-truth, half-lie. The ways of man seem so good to him; he is loathe to relinquish them to see the truth.

The little book of laws that dominate man and dictate the time or age to which the works of man are bound[64] cannot be received by those who believe they are wise. It can only be received by those who wish to give up all their thoughts and opinions to the all-wise Creator. It is He who can make sense of these things to willing hearts.

---

[64] See Revelation 10.

To all those who believe they must hang onto their old beliefs and understandings of the Bible I ask these questions, "What is it worth to you to know the Truth as it *really* is? Would you prefer to keep your own ideas if you knew you were holding truth in contempt?" In his foolishness, man fights to preserve his evil ways of reason and of judgment which are darkened even more by the overarching abominations in the systems of the beast.

To all of you trained in Christianity, those followers of creeds and dogmas – who are you following beyond your own pre-set ideas, habits, and formats? What do you seek to accomplish by holding to your own ways, heaping spite upon Truth? And who will speak for Christ and God if all men seek to keep their views because the truth did not suit them?

The Pharisees sought to crucify and kill Me because I was exposing their wickedness and threatening their supposed power of reason. Yet how little your reason is worth compared to the greatness and ongoing journey of God's great purpose and truth. You will not be a part of this journey, nor understand it, unless you conform to it and hide in the shadow of its wings.

Almighty Peace has come to rid the world of sin, sickness, and death, all of which come through man's will – not God's. And look what man's will creates – selfishness, sickness, disbelief, and destruction. Why is it so easy to insist on your own beliefs, all of which are formed from your conception of truth, yet so difficult for you to give up your knowledge and allow yourself to be guided as a child by the Infinite Wisdom? Open to that Wisdom, go where It leads you, grow as It directs you to see and believe, work as It shows you how to be successful, and know that such work is eternal in force.

Search yourselves and know that you have not come to "bible college" where you can accept what you like and discard the rest. You have come to Life Eternal, Himself, and He holds out a bowl of bread to you. Will you challenge Him because it is not as you expected?

If necessary, I will reveal Myself to you more slowly, that you may think clearly and willingly receive. I question only the motive within that seeks to hold to the old while reaching forth to receive the new. The new cannot be contained in old bottles, nor mixed, because then all will be marred. Therefore, give yourself to all and let Me pick and choose what shall remain or go, because you do not have the wisdom to do this. We can go more slowly so that you may deal with your altars to pride in religious knowledge, for you do not know the hold it has on you, nor the vastness of your ignorance that must be overcome. Practice seeing Me in My perfect love, and believe Me as *I Am* for I will not lie to you.

You have not yet seen Me as *I Am* or truly understood what I have given you. Nevertheless, work to make yourselves worthy through willing surrender to My Holy Spirit. Seek to receive its guidance, which is and will always be perfect and complete. Submit your thoughts to Me for sorting that I may pick and choose among them, discarding the old so they can be replaced by the new law and order of Creation. I love you, My Creatures, and more than you know, I want you to receive and understand My instruction. Let it wash away your dross.

Your meetings are of great significance because they birth My Sons and Daughters. I will teach a nation through a newsletter. Seek to be a part of truth and add nothing which smacks of darkness or of your own mind or experience, only that which I give you, fresh and current, in the meeting. My people have a great need to hear the Truth and I cannot give them the wisdom of man to eat, but must infuse them with Purity and Life.

Surrender yourself to My guidance and hold nothing so dear that I cannot change or rearrange it, otherwise I must take it away, but I will not leave you without vision. *Vision equals understanding.* The pillars of man's beliefs and ideas shake and tremble. They are ready to fall at the advent of My Truth. In the face of Truth everything will fall, including those who believed the old beliefs. Come! Submit your reason and your knowledge. I, the Refiner, will burn away the will of the flesh world as you come and submit these to Me.

#2 The basis of all thought is rooted in the SELF and how you can further your own pleasure, advantages, self-worth, etc. The ROOT of all your troubles comes from focusing on your *self* and not Me. I created you as a child of God, a child of promise, and gave you a will to use either for Me or against Me. People everywhere think they are *for* Me and working hard to follow My Laws and establish My Kingdom on earth – but all they are doing is serving themselves. The only way they can learn My Laws and build My Kingdom is by becoming quiet and going inside to find what I reveal to them. Men and women just do not know that they are *all* wrong. They go about setting up formidable minds as a "task force" or "blue ribbon committee" – and only make the problem worse.

Listen and know that I bring forth DIVINE REVELATION in order to bring men to the end of their self-will and let them see that they are on the brink of total paganism while practicing so-called Christianity.

All those who are interested in My words and in doing My work, Come! and ponder carefully what I say, for the world of man that is not according to My Laws will be destroyed. O man, your whole system of religions and governments will know their end along with those within Christendom that embraced its laws, creeds and dogmas.

Be aware! It is time to save your souls from My judgment.

#3 The rocket of God's purpose will blast away every opposition of man. The show-offs will be broken and transplanted into fallow fields where they will learn to be humble plants. Otherwise, as weeds and vines, they will overrun My entire garden and mar its beauty and perfection. As long as man is given a free will to choose for himself, he will be fallible and prone to mistakes. Therefore, I reserve for Myself proper judgment. My decisions are *not* hard and fast, so I may change them.

I must have perfection in My governing classes. And if one vessel is marred because of being too thick or too thin to bear the strain I had planned for it, then I must remake it. To do this, it must be laid aside. I have a good many other replacement vessels that have been set aside. Some are only half-formed and hardened in that condition, and they do not know why they were left to harden, half-worked. But I have set them aside in case I need them, in which case I will work them like a new vessel I was making that simply became marred in My hand.

Like the clay upon a wheel, you think you have *nothing* to do with My framing of you. But you can be too hard and dry and unworkable and thus I must discard you completely into a bucket of water for awhile. Obedience is like pliability. Yet stiffness or softness are needed at varying times, and that kind of clay is useful to Me. And thus I work, making vessels that seem to both honor and dishonor Me.

Understand that every vessel has its own free will that I will not overstep, forcing it to change and be what I need it to be. However, those who won't change become vessels of dishonor, fit only for a destructive purpose.

Signed,

The Potter

#4 Blessed is the day the Lord comes forth and claims you for His own. His Light is in you and on the ground He sows. He has prepared His soil for planting. He is ready for growth and a bountiful harvest. You are the seed He has prepared for planting.

My Children, you are all at different levels in this season of good planting. No man knows what I will plant in the garden of My delight nor will any man know where in the garden I have planted the seeds of good pleasure which will be a treasure in Heaven when harvested from your earth kingdoms.

Some of My Seeds are now ready to be planted in good ground. They have been hard and dry; dormant in Me. I shall put them in My furrows and cover them with My nutrients. I will cry My rain upon their fields and deeply water them until they emerge from their hardened shells, descending to put forth a firm root and ascending upward as their tender shoots break the crust of their captivity.

My fields are tended by My most faithful servants who delight in the growth and blessing of these Little Ones. My servants rejoice in My triumph over the captivity. They see how much tenderness is necessary to protect My tender plants. We make sure that they are not trampled or broken until My strength is established in their stems.

I will fertilize My fields with every good thing necessary for My Little Ones. I am like a doting parent protecting them, not allowing a single harm to enter in as they continue to grow in Me, by Me, and through Me.

My garden is at many levels of completion. Some plants are ready for harvest. Some plants are newly found tender shoots breaking forth. Some are seeds already planted in Me. Others are seeds being planted this day. I give the nourishment of My Light and My Power equally to all. I will complete My task fully in each as the growing season continues into harvest. Some seeds grow quickly; others take longer to reach maturity. I, who know all things, know when to plant each that all might harvest together as One in Me, in My good season.

Blessed be He who plants. Blessed be He who sows. Blessed be He who tends and weeds the good garden of the Lord.

#5   If, after all this time, you do not know what I am bringing forth, then you must go back and again read all that I have given recently so that the picture will be clear to you.

If you read it too fast, thinking only to grab the knowledge without really understanding, or without turning its Light upon yourself in order to expose and eliminate your darkness, then you were in too much of a hurry. Perhaps you wanted to find fault with another, so you threw the Light of Truth upon him rather than the beast within your own bosom. If this is the case, then you will be unchanged by the Heat and Light of My Truth. This is nothing more than judging, and beware – you will be judged as capable of nothing more than those you judge as less than yourself.

O foolish man! How dare you judge and condemn your brother when you are in a similar but *worse* condition. The loose and immoral man gives himself a high seat that I have not given him. He takes up a gavel and gives out a verdict from his own heart of wickedness within. He judges another and then hands out punishment, asking you to help administer this or that sentence, whether through whippings by the tongue or purging by the lash of another kind.

O foolish man! The judgment you make on others is what will befall you. The pit you have made and tried to cast your brother in will devour you instead! Perfection of judgment and understanding of all implications is given only to Me. No judgment should be given by man to his brother man because I have made you all EQUAL, not one high and another low. All judgment must proceed from above; otherwise it will not be a right use of judgment based in truth. It will end up being some form of scorn, envy, injustice, or jealousy, and certainly it will contain earthly, sensual, and devilish wisdom.

Do not allow yourself to operate in the lower forms of consciousness, but come into higher consciousness! This is where man ceases to see other men, his brothers, in scorn and contempt. This is where it is possible to see that you have also been worthy of judgment and punishment by a DIVINE SOURCE. This is where mercy is found, and your brother is no less worthy of the same mercy. Heed My words and listen to My admonishments for they are Spirit and Life, and if used properly, they will deliver you from repeated death. If used improperly to beat and abuse your brothers, then it will be in yourself that death works its sentence.

Every man is to examine himself in the light of My Truth. If he passes judgment off of himself or deems himself above reproach and therefore infallible, he is caught in pride. If he hardens and cannot move himself to a place of humility and contriteness, he is not useful and must be broken and removed for further cleansing of impurities. This is My work among men.[65]

#6 My Sons, within the depths of your individual soul offer Me your *trespass offering*. Each of you has trespassed against your brother by judging him to be wrong, stupid, lazy, dishonest, or having some other quality that does not honor him. In doing so, each of you has trespassed against My Grace. I will judge *you* according to the measure of your transgression unless you change your attitude and offer love and forgiveness to your brother. Based on the measure of your offering to him *and how sincere your offering is,* I will forgive you according to what you have offered him.

These trespasses must be cleaned away as filth must be washed from your cup. Who would fill his cup with filth and then drink it? I, your Redeemer, am offering to fill your cup with My Holy Drink, but I will not fill vessels that refuse to be cleansed. Your souls are parched and thirsty; you are in need of what I offer. Those vessels unwilling to come to Me clean and open must, in due season, be

---

[65] Romans 12 is a simple, clear, and beautiful description of model behavior for those who want to practice the spirituality of higher consciousness, as well as humility and charity to all.

discarded, for they will not be fit for use and for the good purpose which I have ordained in My heart of grace to those I have called.

All who do not answer the horn when it sounds shall be reassigned to another duty. So in this new day of My Reign, give your calling back to Me so that your election to My fold is affirmed and sure.

Let he who has eyes see and he who has ears hear the intent of My instruction, which is to purify the mixture in the camp. I will see what and how you do in this task, and I will only use those who are fit and usefully employed on My behalf.

Surrender all in quietness, and I will show each of you, as I think you are able to receive, My judgment of your condition at this time. Do not consult among the congregation, for I deal now with individuals only. Do not let the right hand know what the left hand does or whether it is extended or withdrawn.

These things I do are for your own good, not to your detriment or condemnation, for I deal now in mercy. Judgment will be reserved for those who do not pay attention to the sound of My Trumpet as it blasts throughout the camp.

#7   Lest the all-inclusive scope of Calvary escape you, remember I died for all equally, no less for some than for others. And what sin is greater than any other? All sin means you have *separated yourself from Me and are pursing your will rather than God's will in you.* That separation will bring *barren, fruitless decay.*

So hear Me, all of you who find yourselves in this condition. You cannot judge by *how long* you pray or what you do outwardly, but rather by the *sincerity of heart with which you give your whole self to Me.*

If there are idols in your heart, you will not be flexible enough to do what I ask. If you have treasures locked away inside you that you feel are important, you will not allow My Light to expose the Truth to you. Thus, I will not be able to soften you enough to correct you. This can only happen when I am held as the King of kings in your heart and your life.

Those who secretly worship their idols must remain locked away in their hardness. Their attitudes, ideas, and concepts of what is important and how life should be will remain untouched by My hand. Let all who are set in their ways re-think their life or else their state of hardness will result in their being left behind to serve their idols. I will find others to do My work, people who are more fit for the task.

No vessel has an absolute destiny. The choices open to My Children change as they let go of the old self, and this will continue to be so for all, until the seat of your inner authority has been filled by Me and you begin to witness for Me. Know and understand that I have always kept replacements handy to carry on My work in My most important places.

I have never said a man could not fall from the place I have ordained for him, for this is exactly what will happen if he is serving himself more than Me. I require *all* My servants to place their calling upon My Altar. This keeps them from holding it so tightly that they cannot let it go if I require it. The greatest threat to any calling is the self-satisfaction of having "attained" it and thinking you do not need to change any more. This hardens the heart and mind into a pattern of pride and judging others, while putting off all the corrections needed for the self.

Therefore beware, all you who follow Me and think you have attained high status. I will not hesitate to show you another way than the one I first chose for you. If you harden yourself, you commit a first offense. But if you continue to avoid being flexible, you make your sin immense.

So listen all you humble Ones! It will be best for you to stay humble. The direction which I first showed you is the way we will continue to go. Do not let your heart become hard, inflexible, and blind, for doing so only complicates things for you. See that I am changing you and will come to your defense.

April 12, 1996

One Lord, One Chief, One Shepherd

HEAR O ISRAEL![66] The Lord Your God is *One Lord.* Your Commander in Chief is *One Chief.* I am not two or three or four or more. Understand that no man is to govern you but ME ALONE! Instead of looking to man or men to be strengthened, become silent and listen to the COMMANDER WITHIN. He is the One who will be Chief in battle and wise in your wars.

The *I Am* will guide you moment by moment, and you will not follow orders dictated by men because *you are all in the same boat and fallible!*

If you try to make yourself look or sound important, you will be deposed. Where you strengthen your arms of flesh or rely on the wisdom of man, you will fall. And where you trust in man, you will be disappointed. Pay attention to GOD ONLY! This is My command to all My people.

---

[66] This is not a reference to the nation of Israel that currently exists in the north of Africa. When broken into its constituent parts, *Is Ra El*, the *Is* has to do with eternal existence, *Ra* refers to those who exist in the Light and who consciously reflect a particular ray of that Light, and *El* is a term that denotes the highest form of god-consciousness possible while still able to be an individual human encased in matter.

What Man or Organization Can Stand Against Me?

My Sons and Daughters, this is what the *I Am* says to you…

Who is the man, the organization, who can withhold the floods of blessing I send you? With what will they dam up My raging torrent? By what mechanism will they control the floods of truth sent to your parched land? Woe to all who try to "administer" My reign within My Kingdom, which I created for good purpose and pleasure. The torrents of truth will leave all the old ways, the old customs, the old teachings unsettled and cast away, never to be found. In this day I again create anew, creating by My desire, by My plan, and I do not consult or consort with the worldly powers who were taking My place as if I were sleeping, unmindful of their doings and the effects of those doings. There is no damage that they have done which I Am cannot straighten! To their consternation and confoundment, I Am will show them and tell them this: the I Am is alive and well and will be so forever. They will see thunder and lightning as I arise, and will tremble as I arrive to reclaim all that is mine!

April 17, 1996

Change Must Begin

The time has now come for change to begin in the earth. You have known and seen changes happening already, but nothing like what is just ahead. Prepare your hearts and minds to be fully anchored in Me, for if you are not, the rapid changes will sweep away the weak ties you think will adequately hold and secure you against any storm. I am coming to deal with every man, woman and child upon the earth. See that you do not harden your hearts.

Listen and obey My voice of instruction. Prepare quickly; the battle has already begun. I, Your Lord and Redeemer, the One who holds all things in His hands, am giving you more grace, love and power than you have ever had before. Do not be dismayed by the trials, tests, or the battle, for where sin abounds, grace abounds even more. Reach up, receive, and walk the path I have provided for you!

Pray and Stay Alert

WOE! WOE! WOE unto mankind! The forces of nature have been let loose on them. The earth is full of idolatry. I have pleaded and pleaded but man fails to listen. Many more will have to lose their lives. I will not condone their wickedness much longer. Too many innocent victims are caught in their web and cry for help.

Yes, the culprit is Christendom. Far too long she has played the harlot. No more. She is to be exposed by My Sons and Daughters who have followed My Truth. Listen carefully My Children, it is time for a great explosion. Pray and stay alert for My instruction. Soon we will be shouting the song of victory. Be cautious, My Loved Ones, The Beast seeks to devour you. Look around you. My angels are ready to strike. ◆

April 19, 1996

The "Resurrection Sunday" Experience Results in New Birth

My little flock, today I have shown you confirmation flowing in upon My handmaiden, the wind, that I am doing a new thing here in this place. My New Pentecost will send raging torrents of truth from you, My manifested Sons and Daughters. I will send heavenly wisdom to you and *through* you as My precious words. These will be words your world has never understood or thought about.

Man has not seen or imagined the gifts the *I Am* bestows since the beginning of this Age. This is My New Day. Let the floodgates of Heaven be opened to you this day so Truth can cleanse all. My new dispensation of Truth and Light will not be open to debate by men, for all of the inhabitants of your world will see and know this Truth as the *I Am* rises in power and holy glory in you. Your world will stand in wonder, captured by the majesty of My New Day!

I have declared that your New Day begins with the resurrection of your souls to Me, by Me, and through you the *I Am* of old awakens. So wipe the slumber from your eyes and stretch yourself into the newness to which the *I Am* has called you. I call you individually, that the Truth of My Light might begin to shine in you and reveal how close you are to awakening the Christ within. Let My words of fire cleanse you and reveal to each of you the blight of that period when you were caught in the life of the low self.

Today, when you return to your private closet of study, examine yourself carefully. Are MY WORDS nearby, far off, or are they lost to your command? You alone, with the truth of My pure wisdom, can determine your present position. Can your mind grasp My last twelve newsletters? My last ten newsletters? My last seven newsletters? Or maybe only the last three? Be honest with yourself and you will know the fullness of your stewardship over what I have taught you. Then we can determine how much passion you have as a student of My Truth.

If My words are not the greatest of treasures to your soul, then how might I convince you? How can My light shine within you, and where could you go to gain the growth to which I have called you? I ask each of you to conduct this examination of yourself, and then I will deal with and heal you of whatever we might find. I, your Redeemer, will not attempt to criticize or condemn, I will simply try to expose your weaknesses and sins to you that you may correct them.

This is a new day of enlightenment for My little flock. The *I Am* is with you and says to you, *"The old is gone. Do not bring it with you into this new day. My mercy and grace is now in and around you so that your former life can be made anew."*

You are new creatures in Me and by Me; and through Me, each of you will be endowed and illumined by the fullness of My Light in your individual lives. My new Pentecost will roar like a mighty wind around all you who tarry with Me, inwardly waiting for Me to fill you daily with pure direction from Holy Spirit. The effect of My inner Light removes the shades from the windows of your heart. It opens the windows wide and allows My pure air to shine away the staleness of the occupation of your old self-man.

Your soul will no longer be tormented as you progress toward Me, and you will be greatly refreshed and your hope nourished as you begin to grow into full maturity as My Sons and Daughters. *I will come forth from your deepest Self.* The Light of Truth will utterly flood the darkness that surrounded you and kept you captive and imprisoned by the habits and beliefs of your former self-man. That old self will be cast away and cut asunder within you and will never bother you again. You will be made completely new. Your eyes will not see as before, but will focus in a singular way on what My Spirit within you reveals to you. You will see many wondrous and marvelous things as you are edified completely by Spirit's plan and purpose. Your ears will be flooded with melodies of My communion with you to guide and instruct you. I will lead you and you will hear Me as a rushing river of refreshment flowing into a dry world, as My words resonate in you, My Children, and you share them with your brothers and sisters. You will be astonished as you lead them, not to yourself, nor to any other man, but to Me. Great shall be the blessing for all who come fully to Me this day.

Many promises have been reserved for My little flocks, but we always begin by cleansing, purging, and setting aside everything from your outside life. That way I can guide you to full maturity. You will be My pattern and I will fashion you into complete Christs. When everyone has reached higher consciousness and the higher dimensions, then we will proceed to demonstrate the fullness of My revelation to the rest of the world.

I call on each of you to re-read all of My words you can find in the privacy of your study. Each time you read them I will show you a *new* thing; you will have a new and deeper understanding. Today I put within you, individually, a new light of understanding, a new level of appreciation, and new ideas for application. Do not deny yourself the richness of your reward by delaying or thinking, "This does not apply to me." ALL MY WORDS ARE FOR THE GROWTH OF ALL SONS AND DAUGHTERS AND FOR THEIR DELIVERANCE INTO THE FULLNESS OF CHRIST-CONSCIOUSNESS VIA PURITY. Hold onto My words, cling to them as if they were balm for your soul, for by them you live in Me and I live in you.

This day My joy is complete in you. Your humility causes even Me to delight in the good work I am doing in you. It is by you and through you that I will send My Light to illuminate the world. My

Love will fill your brothers and sisters, and My Truth will resurrect all of you.

Rejoice and be filled with rivers of joy. Tarry with Me as My Holy Spirit continues to work in each of you, completing your salvation. My garden will spring forth with you as my tender plants, and soon all will be ready for full harvest and the radiant Light of our Father. Amen and Amen.

Again I say, feel My Joy within your souls and allow My wellspring to fill you and satisfy you from the Fountain of Love that reigns within you!

Here and everywhere, humble yourself before Me, your Creator, and before your brother who is also part of My Body. Forgiveness must reign and peace be established.

You do not know how important the principle of loving, sharing, and forgiving is. Remember, as a body has many parts yet is ONE Body, you are together as ONE Body, ONE Church, in Me. And all men will know you are Mine *if you love one another and are kind and affectionate towards one another.* This is the way and manner of those who are attuned to higher consciousness.

When you feel the need within to apologize to a brother or sister, do not wait to do so, for you do not know the stumbling block that it lays before you and your brother's feet, for whom also I died. Therefore, when you bring your gift before Me, if I remind you of something in which you have offended your brother or sister, leave your gift and go make amends with your brother, then return and offer your gift to Me. That way, both yourself and your gift will be acceptable in My sight.

૭૪

This is the season of your rebirth. When you look into the mirror each morning as you awaken, do not see yourself; see only ME, for *I Am* within you and all around you with My arms outstretched, embracing, and wrapping you with My Love. Let it shine forth from you.

Do not let your attention be drawn to the flaws you see in yourself. Be aware that the Light that exposes your mistakes also changes you. I am fashioning you into vessels of My pleasure, and I do not see your lumps of clay because I see you as you will be when I have completed My good work within you. Then I will fire you in My Furnace of Truth until all your weaknesses and hindrances are forgotten. I will adorn you with the beauty of words and actions that are pure and focused on Me. You are a great treasure in the storehouse of Me and My Father, your maker.

Do not be dismayed by that which seems to hold you back. Remain still and watch, and you will see these obstacles go, one by one, until there are none left to hinder your complete salvation.[67] I complete whatever I start, and so it will be with you as My work is done within you. *Let yourself* be of good cheer and be filled with joy.

I long to give My Children every good thing. A child can only receive at one level and can only digest at an elementary level. I want all of you to grow unto full brotherhood in Me. Then I can show you *a secondary enlightenment* where you and I can commune and feast upon the treasures of heaven. We will be as one, equal in stature before our Father. As equal Sons, we will discourse in word and deed throughout eternity.

Right now, in your world, many seek but go only part way to Me because doubt and fear puts distance within your hearts. Some

---

[67] *Salvation* means you have stopped believing that this world is Real or that material reality is all that exists. When you get this far, you can detach from things a bit and begin saving yourself from the troubles and drama that you used to create in your life because you were so tangled up in it. This leads to being able to see that you are not subject to the world and can begin to allow the Christ within to guide you toward the reality of the heaven worlds, which is one of peace, joy, brotherhood, love, abundance, and life that does not have to contend with death any more.

give only 30-fold. Others are drawn to Me 60-fold. But I long for 100-fold to be achieved in each of you. When the manifestation of My illumination comes to My First Fruits group, the New Jerusalem Church will be birthed in glory and radiant Light here on the earth. It will be a pattern and blessing of My fullest rewards. Then the 30-fold and the 60-fold will be drawn in to complete My Grace.

The heart is a precious treasure and is the center of joy for those who reach the highest consciousness. *You are an individual kingdom and in your kingdom your heart is the THRONE of Christ.* Satan, who works through the low self, also covets the throne of your heart that he may rule selfishly from there, to the destruction of many. You do not know the many tricks and ways he has of side-tracking your progress in Me. My admonition to you is to lay your life upon My altar and die to the little opinions and prejudices that crop up every day, in order that you may confound all Satan's designs, which you won't even notice if you keep your eye set on Me.

If you are watching and waiting to be tempted, you will indeed fall. If you rely on your own strength, you will find you do not have enough of it to overcome the temptations. But by keeping your eye and your heart fixed on Me, temptation will come and go unnoticed, and you will remain unsullied by it.

Therefore, with Me in front of you, keeping your mind quiet, free of disturbing thought, and very still, holding My true and holy Church without spot or wrinkle, know that you only find My way hard when you struggle to make the world follow Me, which cannot be done. Fix your eye upon Me and do not even glance at the temptations the world offers you. Do not allow yourself to be drawn into vanity over how well you are doing either. This way you will remain quiet and pure in Me. You will be immersed in a HOLY LOVE AFFAIR with Me, one in which you should hold Me above your love and desire for any creature in your world.

If you think you do not have this kind of love, ask Me for it. Go after it with all the strength and desire you can muster and you will find it. As you sow in the spirit instead of in the flesh, you will reap a bountiful harvest of Love, for I am the Author of Love.

The Wellspring From On High pours forth rivers of Living Water to bring you deliverance. It washes away the confusion of the flesh and evil. Each day My Life issues from Me to the hungry, and My Water of Life and Truth flows to the thirsty. *Receive and give My Bread and Water of Life to everyone around you.* If you do, I will bless you because you allow yourself to be used for your brother's sake.

Wherever you go and in all times and places, I will be a Wellspring of Life within you, pouring the words of life and hope to you in your need. As you empty out yourself, I will fill you with an abundance of Me. Where you hold back in fear, you will see that there is a great price for this, and you will be able to measure your distance from Me by seeing the price and the effects of that fear.

By drawing closer and *letting go of the things that separate you from your desire for Me*, you will be purified and cleansed of all that creates the distance and idolatry in your life. No, you do not worship idols in the form of statues, but you do worship the people, houses, careers, money, power, and status that you think will save you and make you happy. This is your idolatry, and these are the things you hang onto in your hearts, worshipping them and acting as if they will give you Life.

O My Children, let there be no idols to replace Me. Hang a picture on your wall to remind you that *I Am* is the Lord or Lady of your Life and rules over your individual kingdom. Ask yourself, do you truly want My Kingdom to come to you and My Will to be done in you as it is done in the heaven world? If yes, then focus your heart and your life on Me. Completely release your burden of cares, hopes, wishes, dreams, and even your goals. Commit yourself to following

My Will rather than yours and let me watch over you and keep you safe.

I want a holy group of people totally committed to Life in Me, for through you My wonders can flow out to the rest of My people. You are My examples to the world, My First Fruits group. I say this with utmost sincerity and seriousness, and I know it comes with a price – everything that you have and all that you are. Each one of you becomes like a sacrifice on the altar of your heart as you place Me in front of you and look to Me in love. Do not do this out of duty but rather out of love for your brothers and sisters who will watch you and hope these things can be done, but who cannot reach My Higher Consciousness until they see others have done so.

Will you obey Me completely? I see many cringing even yet. I know how PRECIOUS your sacrifice to Me is! I know how great the treasure of your heart is when offered to Me! All of heaven rejoices when you offer it, for you are Mine, and they are Mine, and you and they are ONE together in Me.

Your brothers and sisters in the heaven worlds rejoice at your progress like a great cloud of witnesses who watch over you day and night and love to intercede for you.[68] They are your ancestors, your forefathers whom you do not know. They walked with Me before you. You are their seed that I continue to bless because of their walk and right use of their consciousness. Their joy will be full because of your obedience. You have been cut from the same rock as they and of the one immortal seed of Christ, thus you will be re-united as one heavenly body with them.[69]

Cast aside the worries and sins that the world beckons you to follow. Let nothing hinder you in this race that you run to your own

---

[68] See Hebrews 12:1-15

[69] See Isaiah 51:1-9 for a rousing description of how the nations and kingdoms of men and material things will pass away swiftly while the Kingdom of God, aka "heaven," remains steady, strong, and ongoing.

individual finish line. Understand that you triumph or fall not for yourself only, but for all those who wait to be re-united with you.

Let your joy be full. Let your peace be complete. Through humility, through patience with both good times and difficult times, by completely re-thinking how you want to live your Life, and then re-organizing it by letting go of your old self, a new life can be formed in you.

I will bring you forward through levels and degrees of surrender, helping you to learn obedience in one level before the next level is entered into. This work must be done, either on this side of death or on the other. Do it now so you can obtain Life and eternal Joy on the other side.

No levels and steps can be missed, for there are certain tests and lessons to be learned. If you are obedient, we go forward. As you stumble or lag behind, you hold back your whole group.

If it were up to Me, I would advance you all every week. Instead, I must limit My blessings to those who are obedient, and I must continue to teach those who hold back or stumble. Therefore, pay attention to yourself so that you are not just lazy and hinder the entire group.

I will fulfill My promise to those that walk with Me and you, showing the entire nation through you as My examples. At first they may feel ashamed, but then they might discover their own humility and be encouraged to pick up their own cross by letting go of old thoughts and ideas and following Me. And yes, they will need you as examples.

My People, keep your mind and thought on Me! I say this over and over! The children of Israel were disobedient and grumbling over My provisions. They provoked Me to My face, so I was angry with them and sent forth venomous serpents. Yet even as they were bitten, I had My Servant, Moses, erect a brazen serpent which, if they looked at it, would heal them of their bites.

I tell you this because I want you to see that even in the midst of your sin and the resulting death that works in you, I can restore Life and Peace to you. Thus, *focus upon Me and you will live.* You will rise up and go forward with your life. As long as you keep your eyes on Me, you will continue to be victorious.

I am the Most High, and the strength of your commitment can be found in Me. Without Me, you are nothing, and all of you are subject to death through your ignorance. Yet I am here to tell you that the *I Am* will lead you and bring you to Myself, the Christ within you. Whatever your commitment and diligence is, that is what will be for you.

Depending on how much you will release yourself to Me, you will reap the rewards 30-fold, 60-fold, or 100-fold. I will fill you with what lasts forever. Your mind will be on eternal things, not temporal things. Your steps will be eternally guided and the path will be plain for you to see because My Light will light your path. If you do not seek My Guidance, you will walk in darkness and dwell in a world where death comes eventually to all.

What I say to one, I say to all: *Seek Life. Seek peace and pursue it. Pay attention to what you do with your consciousness. Correct it in all ways so you will continue to walk with Me, for that is its purpose – to lead you to My ways. I know how the world of men can mislead you. I died to show you My Comforter and to demonstrate that you do not have to believe you are subject to death. You can learn to live in such a way that you will live forever. Therefore, Come to Life! Come out of your tombs of dead thinking, O My People! Let go of what you have learned from the world of men. Go into the closet of your private self and begin communicating with Me. Do not stop until you have found Me, and when you have grasped Me, never let go. Do not go back into believing human teachers or what you see in the world. Let Me teach you, Myself, and lead you, Myself, and raise your consciousness to the highest level, Myself, until you are quiet, clean, and renewed. Then you will be fit for My purpose just like the ones I am sending these words through. So watch and listen! Watch and know My way. And do not leave My way lest you again become ensnared by the habits and traditions of the world. I am giving you hope. I am giving you Me, and I pray that you will turn to your Maker in all things. Amen.*

I call to you, My Children, who are in the tombs of the dead. Awaken, arise, and move forward with your new Life in Me. Can you see that I have come to you through these words to resurrect you to a new Life and free you from the chains of death that have held you captive? Are My words any less effective because you do not *see* Me? No, for as I proclaim, so it is.

I will bury all opposition to My Plan and Purpose, and My immense radiance will come forth. All those who live as if they are dead will hear My Voice and begin moving toward a new Life.

Listen to Me, My Children, for I have not forgotten you. Turn your face to Me, not your back, and do not serve the gods that the world puts in front of you. The *I Am* within you is the One God you are to worship and honor and there is no other. I know not any. Rejoice that I have called you. Heed that call and arise from the tombs of your houses, your stale and sterile lives. I will make the barren wilderness of your hearts into fruitful fields. When I say "fruitful," I am not referring to works of man or the world that bring no joy or Life. I am referring to the fruits of Spirit and all abundance, which pleases My Father. Thus, see that your fruit continues through the fires of My testing, which happens to everyone, to see if he is truly committed to Me.

There is much work to do in this world, and you become so busy doing it that you have no time to seek Me, to feel Me flowing inside your hearts and minds, to receive My guidance and to know My plans. This is why so much of the work done in the world by the will of man is neither pleasing, nor beneficial, let alone eternal and everlasting. They do not seek Me or My Will and thus they cannot withstand My Fires.

All of you servants, striving to do something you have decided to do for me – *stop your laboring!* You can deliver no one, not even yourself, unless and until that deliverance has been sanctioned by Me, orchestrated by Me, and led by Me. And I will not do these things until you have prepared yourself and are ready, willing, and worthy to do them in accord with My Will.

There is no real and lasting Life except through the death and letting go of your old ways. I know this sounds confusing and complex to your mind. But think of yourself as the butterfly, who by going within and transforming itself has found new life – a winged life! In that same way you can find winged life in Me – but only through transformation of your former self.

A seed in a jar remains alone, dry, and dormant until the day it is put into the ground – buried – and dies to what it was. But then it sprouts with a multitude of new potentials and grows to be very fruitful. The form of the seed has sacrificed its wants, its desires, its dry loneliness for a future that results in a better life for all. This is true for you, O My seeds of glory. Within you is the same potential to bring forth much life to many, if you are willing to die to what you are, that the Christ might come forth in you as a new type of Being, full of radiant Light, full of holy Power, full of healing Power, Power that you can share with the nations. Can you see that you, the leaves of My trees of *right-use-ness*,[70] will be agents of healing for whole nations?

You see yourselves as small and weak and ask what could *you* possibly do. But if even one of you can transform yourself, you will see how one can change thousands! *One* obedient one can create

---

[70] The term "right use of" is usually spoken as *righteousness* and refers to the fact that when we listen to the still, small voice of the Christ within, we will always be right in our choice of words and actions and will nurture *Life*. Nurturing *Life* is the right use of our time, energy, and power.

so much good! But you will not see it unless you enter My consciousness and let the flow of Life itself teach you how to obtain eternal Life and joy.

When the difficult times come, call upon Me, My Children. When you need Me the most, call upon Me. I am the Redeemer of your heart. O My Children, call upon Me, so My Rain of mercy will flow to you. My Love for you is everlasting and will remain in you so that you may complete My Work. Call... call... and I will surely come.

Your heart will be made into a pure vessel filled with My Radiant Light for all. How good and precious it is for a heart of love to demonstrate My Truth and Love to all generations! What a prize to Me! A willing heart and a ready pen, a soul seeking to be useful and help bless his brethren, mankind – no earthly value can be placed upon it, yet in My Kingdom its value is beyond measure.

You are more precious than gold or diamonds or all precious stones. Yet in yourselves you see no good. If you think that is true, offer Me what you have. Regardless of how big or small, I will know how to design it, to take the usefulness of it and use it for the betterment of all mankind.

※

O holy people, CONSECRATE ALL YOU ARE TO ME AND ALL YOU HAVE FOR MY USE. Let your sacredness be purified in this way.

Parents, from your heart give Me the lives of your children for My Service. Let go and let Me have them back so I can guide them Myself. They are Mine first. They are only yours to raise in wholeness and purity for Me. Dedicate yourselves and them to My Work *even before you know what it is*, and I will bless your offering many fold, making your hearts glad. Families, you *must* pray together and forgive one another. Do not think that you are more worthy of special consideration than your brothers and sisters.

All My people will one day come to Me and live My way, but I have called you first so that by your example the others will be drawn as well. You are first, and if you are rejected by others – hold onto Me while I lead you, even if you do not know where you are going. You can be confident of one thing, however, that our destiny is the radiant glory of Life lived in the Light.

The essence of power comes through discipline, even when it comes to the Almighty. Power is not given to anyone who judges according to the world's standards, for this would be very destructive. You must develop a heart of mercy, or power will not come forth from you. Until your own obedience is certain and loving, you cannot bring deliverance to others.

With what can you bless Me, Children? There is no greater way to bless your Creator than with your obedience. Words can be meaningless, and many times are, yet actions speak VOLUMES even when you say nothing. So bless Me, Children, with hands and hearts of obedience, for these are among My Treasures.

After you have learned obedience, you are given the power to help many others. So if you seek the power to heal or to deliver others from sorrow and suffering, *lay hold of Life Eternal,* even when it means death to all your own personal judgments, opinions, and ideas of self-worth. When you see yourself as empty, as nothing, then you will be ready for My power to fill you.

Therefore, seek the lowest place as you reach for Eternal Life. You can benefit many who cry to Me from the tombs of their desolation, even from the tabernacles of Christendom, which has become man's best effort at replacing God and worshipping man instead.

Study the fullness of My Spirit within you as you eat from My Table. Spirit will come forward and begin to work in you, and you will discover that the symbolism you were content with before is only a shadow of that which breaks forth in reality. Keep your eye on Me and come to know Me in the Drink of Life and the Bread of Life. I AM YOUR LIFE, and you cannot live simply by eating the necessary foods, but by every word that comes from the mouth of your Eternal Father, God. Amen.[71]

Consider a room that has a light controlled by a dimmer switch. You, too, are a room filled with light that you have controlled by dimming your consciousness. Are you content to get by with only the light of a single candle? Or would you rather have the whole room fully illumined to the extent of its potential brightness? The dimmer switch is in your control, and you have the power to turn My Light on high and full, or turn it down so low you can barely see the carpet. Your willingness to let go of your old ways will turn up the brightness of the room of your heart. Roll up the shades! Flood the room with My Light! Let it chase away all your darkness and despair. Receive Me and My Eternal Light which exists in all of you, My Sons and My Daughters.

The sacrifices of God are a broken heart and a contrite spirit. Though at times it may seem dark and dreary, it will not always be so. The way will open before you, Light will break forth into a new day, and you will see better times. Do not make a God of the past. Let Me lead you out of the darkness you are now experiencing and you will see better times ahead for you.

Greatness is Mine. You are all My Servants, and I love you. I will guide you as you go forth for Me. I long to be *with* you and *in* you. I will direct your paths.

---

[71] The word *amen* is a derivative of *aum,* which is considered to be the "word" of God, and is really the sound created by the great matrix of frequencies that we draw Life from.

Your world is blind. Your world is held captive under the sting and shadow of death. There are no worthy teachers except those who have given themselves to Me so that I might teach and lead through them, prophetically so. They do not teach what is in their own mind nor do they lead you to worship or pray to themselves. They put Me first and see themselves only as instruments in My hand. Therefore, hear Me and listen to what I tell you. A NEW DAY IS DAWNING in your midst, despite where you are and no matter how far away you have wandered. I call you back from the lands of your prodigal ways, back to truly searching your heart, to repentance, even to brokenness that causes you to say, "Restore your joy to us, O Lord, that we might be saved from misery and depression."

By the shores of Babylon you hung your harps and mourned of your captivity, and your harps reminded you to sing. Your song has not been of victory, but of sadness, captivity, and death. Come to me, your Lord, and let me restore the Light that will light your path. The Lord your God is ONE LORD and you have turned your back on Me so you may chase after the personalities of men and hear them instead of seeking to hear Me. You have lost My Voice and drowned yourself in the puke and vomit of man's doctrine and tradition.[72]

If you would turn back to Me, I would have mercy on you, causing your captivity to end and your darkness to be illuminated today. I Am your FIRST LOVE. The Christ has not left you, and you are not without hope or comfort. I have sent My Comforter to guide each of you along the path you should go. But you have despised Him and failed to understand My words concerning Him. You have chosen human teachers over Him and He has fled from you, driven out of your churches by men who SAY they love God, but who only deceive you.

---

[72] Isaiah 28:8 decries the priests and prophets who drink wine in order to have visions and says their words and prophecies are no better than vomit.

My people, how long will you love to wander and choose men's ways over God's? Can men even fathom who God is? Are *they* wise enough to instruct and direct *Him*? Would He be foolish enough to set selfish men over His flocks? Or have wolves entered into My sheepfolds to rape and plunder My sheep for the sake of fame, prestige, and profit?

Be aware and leave Christendom, which is merely of man's making. I will pronounce judgment upon it and it will fall, taking all of man's greatness with it. Do not be mesmerized by the glitz and glamour, for it is putrid with the filth of selfishness and pride.

Hear Me, O World, My Light is breaking forth to illumine your darkness, revealing its reality – the true from the false, the good from the counterfeit. You who stand on the Lord's side, come to Me. Do not stand on the side of Korah and Dathan, who offered my people their golden calf. I will destroy Mammon and all who love it. First there will be the separation of My wheat from the tares which I have allowed to grow together up until My harvest time. Therefore, run to My side and forsake the harlot's houses, if you are My True Wheat. There are no sects or divisions in Me and never will be. But Christendom's kingdom is divided again and again, and it will take a great fall.◆

April 19, 1996

The Vineyard

Have you ever considered the vineyard or how it comes to be? From a vine, the husbandman removes a tender slip, a shoot from the bough. He places it in water until it begins to take root, and then, from one vine comes another of the same. But tender protection is necessary to bring it to full growth. Even though the shoot is ready to plant, it will undergo many strains, many trials, before it can reach maturity. Many shoots are planted before the vineyard can be rich and full. The work of the husbandman is to care for them and watch over them night and day.

Once planted, the soil must be just right. The tender shoot must be placed where it will not be trampled or destroyed by man or beast until it is strong enough to sustain itself in a hostile environment. Then it is necessary to receive the right levels of rain and light. Not too much or too little of either or the shoot will be subject to blight. The shoot cannot do anything to provide for itself or meet its needs, but must submit to the wisdom of the husbandman to see it has proper provisions as it continues to grow into a mature vine.

As the little vine continues to grow, the husbandman must be diligent in caring for the trellis that holds up his tender plant. The plant cannot do this for itself and must trust the husbandman to do so. Years will pass as the husbandman offers loving care. He digs, weeds, and fertilizes, and for some time no harvest has been enjoyed. Still the husbandman toils there caring for the tender plants and maintaining the good ground.

Finally the vineyard comes to maturity and the husbandman is rewarded for his faithful stewardship as his helpless plants become fruitful vines. They share their fruits forevermore. While they were growing, they could give nothing. Now they reward the husbandman with bounty to eat and enjoy.

The Lord is the husbandman, who toils in your fields, caring for you, His tender shoots, His tender plants, for as long as it takes to bring you into full maturity as a Christ. He cries His rain upon you, dries you in His Light, and brings forth your harvest. He alone can do these things for all you can do is be glad and rejoice that your husbandman is faithful to see you through until you are able to reward Him with the goodness of your fruit. As a mature vine, now you, too, provide new and tender shoots, and the husbandman plants them and cares for them. Once again, He is faithful until another level of harvest is added to the one He has currently blessed.

I am the good vine, and you, My Children, are the shoots who are becoming mature vines in My vineyard. Since you came forth from Me, you are of Me and can only bring forth good fruit. I protect you, I nourish you, and I watch over you and delight in your growth toward fullness like Mine. From your vines I replant generations of vines untold. Together we will provide much bounty to feed a hungry world. Amen and Amen.

Heights & Depths

All you who think you dwell on your mountaintops, come with Me, your Redeemer, down into the valley of joy that I might show you that which you see only dimly. Journey with Me and I will provide details to your vision as you watch the handiwork of My hands, presently hidden from you by the distance of your imagined heights. Yes, come with Me, and as we embark upon our journey to that which you regard as *beneath you,* the scales will be removed from your eyes as My understanding is imparted to your souls.

As we descend into the depths, the river that looks like nothing more than a scar upon the land from your lofty perch will appear different. To the inhabitants living in My valley, the river brings life as it flows through flowery fields that you do not know of and cannot see from your house up the mountain. See the dainty tenderness of their leaves as they shimmer in My Light. See their peaceful joy when I shine brightly upon them along My riverside. See the planted fields of crops and grain, humble but necessary for Me to sustain man.

My people live here in the valley of joy. They are obedient and humble in My hand for they know I provide fulfillment of their every need. They are thankful for every drop of rain by which their fields and flocks are maintained. They love what they have been given, which is something the arrogant cannot see or understand. Not until I show it to them can the selfish understand the treasures My people hold nor can they know why My humble ones remain focused upon Me as pure and refined gold.

Now all you who dwell in the valley, come with Me, your Redeemer, to heights that tower far above the mountaintops of your land and I will help you understand something greater.

Yes, everything I've given you is a treasure to hold and I bless you there in your little world. Yet come with Me away from all your material goods and worldly ideas and together we will ascend to an even higher view, one where you can see your greatness, which looks extremely small and can hardly be seen even from up in the clouds.

Up in the heights, you will learn to look up even higher for ever newer blessings, instead of looking down and being content in what little you know. Come higher, says your Redeemer. Leave all that you have in order to receive My wisdom as we pass through clouds of uncertainty and into the certainty of everlasting Truth. Come higher than man has ever seen and together we will behold the unfolding of heaven's dream. Venture into a land where everything is new and untarnished, a place where your vision will see joy upon joy as you are restored to My Sacred Fold.

My Fullness vs. Man's Good Try

Hand Me the fullness you THINK you have, and I will show you the fullness I desire for you. As long are you are proud of the fullness you THINK is fullness, you will never obtain REAL FULLNESS IN ME. Remember, your minds are limited. How can you know fullness, or even what I am talking about, when you see fullness measured by your own insecurities?

I tell you, if you want to see true fullness, look at the Pattern and Example of the Living Christ that lives, moves, and has His Eternal Being through you. He is doing His own work – which you know nothing of and are not capable of doing alone – through your clean, silent, and obedient vessel.

Compare the best effort of your flesh to the Living Christ, and you will then see true fullness versus man's good try.

Spiritual D.N.A. (Does Not Apply)

The inability of man to perceive his own heart is the reason he so easily deceives himself. When he feels he is above scrutiny and is not willing to look within, deception continues until there is a complete overthrow of his heart.

Laymen and women who continually hear sermons that exhort them to examine their conscience keep their mind and eye turned inward.

However, teachers spout sermons and fail to examine themselves in that same harsh light. They have no problem telling others what to do, whether it is critical judgment from themselves or true light from the Spirit. Nevertheless, they must look within themselves because the same tendencies toward weakness become a stumbling block. An intense spiritual pride is set up and the teacher, no matter how "good," is overthrown.

Life, Truth, Emotion, Death

What is *Life*? What is *Truth*? What is *Emotion*? What is *Death* if it is not the "decay of the body in physical death?"

I will give you the answers: *Life* is immortality, *Truth* is our eternal Oneness in Spirit, *Emotion* is movement of energy, and *Death* is separation from Spirit, which results in the decline and death of man.

When Adam and Eve departed from Truth and began their disobedience to My will and My words, they entered into spiritual death. Their sight was veiled, and they could no longer see My Light or My Kingdom. From that point on, they were subject to darkness and were blind to Me and the Father. Spiritual decline set in, and death followed. They did not know that the Tree of Knowledge was poison to their spirit and thought it was only a strange discipline.

Eventually, as more and more of them failed to taste the Tree of Life, they never knew that it was possible to live forever. Soon they forgot their origins altogether and were left trying to understand *death*. They did not know what it was, for they had never seen it.

Thereafter, in their state of death and disobedience, they were unable to participate in My Garden of Eden. As a mercy to them, they were removed from the Garden and then had no chance to eat of My Tree of Life. Why try to live forever and ever when you are caught in the sorrows of man?

My command to you has been obedience to Truth. To teach all truth from one tiny book and think that it is the infallible Word and Authority of the Most High is ludicrous and shortsighted. My Truth speaks *new words for every generation and age*, what was good back in the 1600s will not suffice now in your time and age of existence.

If all the teachings and sayings I gave you during My tenure on earth were to be printed, all the books and libraries in the world could not contain them, so profuse have they been. However, over time My teachings have been sanitized, categorized, colored, and limited as the documents fell into the hands of evil men. The greater part have been destroyed or handed out in meaningless pieces by the churches whose foundations and seat belongs to Satan. At present you have little idea indeed of what I really said, and that little has been perverted in its interpretation.

Further perversion is added when men who know nothing of Me try to teach the remains of My Word for a profit, a name, and a high seat among men. And who is higher in the eyes of most men than a preacher or a priest? Morally speaking – none. They receive great respect and honor, as if they are dreadfully holy. But they do not have the Truth, and they love their honors; thus they suck at the roots of deception.

When emotion takes over and rules the heart, and mental knowledge replaces honest, daily evaluation of one's life, there is no new birth experience. The existence of the soul is threatened when the old "badlands" are simply covered over with external religious commitment. In My eyes, you end up worse off than you were in the first place.

This is why so many Christians experience no inner change, no inward search for truth. They are told that they "have it all" and are to wait in this fashion, keeping their tithes paid, for the future train to Paradise. Once there, they will all receive a pardon – a paid indulgence – along with a heavenly mansion and a gold street with a healing fountain.

But I tell you that to do so or to think so is to make My heaven a hell indeed. The same is true when you merchandise Me and sell My Holy Word, My Holy Dove of Spirit, and My heavenly reward for money.

Woe to those who claim to teach Me for money. They are robbers, thieves, and wolves in sheep's religious clothing! Beware O people of Mine! Come to the ONLY SHEPHERD YOU CAN TRULY TRUST – JESUS CHRIST, HIMSELF. Do not open to any Spirit besides My Holy Spirit, who will not speak of Himself but will take My words and wisdom and reveal it to you personally, and who will individually grow you to maturity in Me.[73]

When I speak of Life, understand that *there is no Life outside of My Holy Substance*. No man can feed you the kernel of Life that he himself received. When you ignore the Essence of Life that runs through you, you are left with only the empty husk of materiality.

If you receive your learning from men, you are cheated. If you return again to men week after week and pay them to bring you to Me, you are foolish. If you reject Me to seek their counsel, you reject Life itself. You search the scriptures with them in an attempt to understand and to find Life, but the scriptures only *talk* about Me, and do so imperfectly.[74]

In all these ways you reject *Life* and choose death, emptiness, and darkness rather than Life and Light. When you choose to follow men and do not keep your eyes on Me, you are double-eyed and double-minded. You are darkness within instead of Light.

---

[73] See the Gospel of John 14:26 and 16:12-15 for gentle encouragement to trust the Holy Spirit and allow It to teach you what you need to know.

[74] See the Gospel of John 5:39-41.

You who revel in man's wisdom are shaky and unstable like waves of the sea, blown and tossed by the changing winds of doctrine. Your house, erected on man's sandy foundation, will collapse beneath you, and all of you who lean on man's learning will tumble and fall, to your dismay.

No other foundation can survive the storms and blasts and gusts that are about to fall on you except the foundation that is laid by Me within you. So all of you living in your house of cards, beware. All of you with your sandy foundations, bewail your coming end, for it is *imminent*.[75] What I say is not to criticize you, but to reveal your true condition and let you see your coming demise if you continue what you are presently doing. So goes My work among the children of men, for I do not want any of you to be lost. My words will save those to whom it is given.

All of you who claim to know Me, if you cannot hear My Words, if you do not have My Spirit of prophecy speaking within, then you are not of My True Church. To join Me, separate yourself from all teachings of man, even books and tapes and gospel songs, for what I do will *uproot* Christendom and destroy all her works. If she has some foothold in you, then you will suffer according to how much you hang onto her. Let go and return to your FIRST LOVE.[76]

You cannot embrace Jezebel and know purity of heart and spirit in Me at the same time. For "Jezebel" is the spirit of the whore who sells her soul for money and false power. She is the spirit of the

---

[75] See 1 Corinthians 3:11 and Matthew 7:24-29 for warnings about what will happen to you if you do not take time to go inside yourself and listen for the Will of Spirit to speak to you personally, rather than following the teachings of men.

[76] Revelation 2:1-5 tells us, "I know all about you, how hard you work and how much you put up with. I know you cannot stand wicked men, and how you tested the impostors who called themselves apostles and proved they were liars. I know, too, that you have patience, and have suffered for my name without growing tired. Nevertheless, I have this complaint to make: you have less love now that you used to." Do not forget to return to *love*.

anti-Christ. If you drink from her cup, you will be drunk and lose yourself in her deception. When her great fall occurs, you will go down with her. Therefore, flee her walls and her deceptive nets while you can, for My judgment falls upon her.

Blindness of Babylon

Blindness is rampant over the whole earth thanks to the churches, both Catholicism and Christendom. They make their converts twice the child of hell that they themselves are. They love their evil ways and do not know the difference between the darkness and the true Light. They call darkness "the Light" and dismiss the True Light as "darkness" or "evil."

If I were to manifest the Christ among them, they would all hurry to commit Me to prison and defame Me as a blasphemer, a treacherous person, guilty of perjury and slander or as many trumped up charges as they could imagine. They would not accept Me now any more than they did back then. They would only hurry to silence Me.

Thus you see the power and authority of the Beast and of mysterious Babylon, the religious harlot. The Beast is the government of men that supports this harlot and protects her. Mean-while she seduces them all. They drink her cup of wickedness and fornication and end up guilty with her in a stand against Truth. Yet in My time, she and they will fall, and it will be a great fall.

Who will allow Me to prepare them? Who will teach them to speak for Me? Who among you is willing to empty out all your own ideas, plans, and goals to be prepared by My hand? Who will allow Me to put My words and wisdom in your mouth to speak up against the Beast and the harlot who lives off the blood of the Saints she has slain in all ages? Watch her judgment come. No one yet knows the extent of it. But if you will let Me, I will prepare you, and we will see the extent of her powers.

The Light upon the True and False Gospels

Watch and know that the acid test you all are about to experience will sift, sort, and categorize all of you. If what you hold reverently cannot withstand My White-hot Fire, it is worthless even if it seems precious and mighty.

So hold on to your worthless beliefs and traditions if you want, but it would be far better for you to release them to Me for My cleansing. Let Me pick and choose, for what you hold dear and revere means nothing if you are deceiving yourself.

You will see the mightiness of Jesus the Christ come forth in *your* day to deliver those who are truly His and to destroy that which is not of Him, even though it is feared or revered by men. The holiness and purity of the Lord is your *true Pattern*, as is His meek and lowly demeanor.

Look at your personality cults and see if there is one bit of humility or "poorness of spirit" among them. Realize, My People, that you are being deceived. Do not give your money to them. Hold your money for My Holy Purpose, as I reveal it to you, for I say You are being robbed and My wrath waxes hot against the robbers of My People. The shepherds of Christendom who claim to be Mine and to speak for Me do so under the dominions and guidelines of the Beast.

Hear Me and understand that I do not reward such giving. Nor do I bless those that "give to get." I have said to you "Do not let your right hand know what your left hand is doing," and I will reward openly what was given in secret.

All you who kindle the fires of worldly desire and encompass yourselves with sparks of self-importance, go ahead and walk in the light of your own fire and the sparks which you have kindled, and you will live in torment and lay down in sorrow.[77]

Peace with God

The peace of God is given to those who practice peace with God and all men. It is not given to those who live and act out of their own self-interest or self-will.

When your worldly self rules your heart and your will, there will be callous attitudes, rebellion, and arguing with God. Disobedience results from a lack of love for God. A lack of respect for His words in order to hold onto your supposed "rights" and have your own way is further disobedience. The result is a lower form of justice that you inflict upon the conscience of humanity.

A willful man cannot hear what God has to say nor can he please God. In all things such a man rules himself and therefore cannot be pleasing in God's sight. In this situation, he will not be at peace within himself, for where self is ruling there is no peace. There are only inner wars and stubbornness against the Spirit of God.

The will of God and the will of man cannot co-exist in the same house. Therefore, where flesh or "self" is entertained and allowed to win the victory, the Spirit of God is cast out onto the trash heap and considered garbage. The human-self gloats in victory and thinks he is wise. However, he is a conceited fool who has cast away his true Self while professing to know and love God.

---

[77] See Isaiah 50:10-11 for a warning about ending up caught in the fires whose flames you have been fanning.

April 20, 1996

The Spirit of Jezebel

The mystery and intrigue surrounding a woman is in the way she constantly changes and in her competition with other women. In order to compete for the attention of her husband's wandering eyes, she must constantly change herself and make herself different.

Now if her husband were a *stable* man with a *faithful heart and steady love* – which is scarcely found among you anymore – things would be different. Instead, men lust after others, and in order to hold his interest, the woman changes her appearance often – and drastically – so as to satisfy his lust.

She would be better off *not changing so often* if she could see that the stability and sameness of her appearance was comforting to him. If she could see that he appreciates who she truly is and how she is, and stopped dressing up to please his eye, then he would be comforted by her presence instead of worried that she is trying to attract some other eye.

You can see the stupidity of men and women. By being so changeable, women keep their men feeling insecure and afraid that they are window-shopping for someone new and showing themselves off. The heart-set of each corrupts everything, but neither knows how to fix it.

A woman who is committed to a man should not dress provocatively, showing off her body, legs, and hair. Neither should a committed man have a wandering eye. Your whole nation is full of adulterous people, and you have not known anything else but captivity to the spirit of whoredom covering your land.

The spirit of Jezebel appears decked in all her fashion finery, with her legs and navel exposed. So many of My Servants who cannot contain themselves stare as she struts by. There are so many temptations right now because Satan knows his time is short *and* he knows where men are weak. Think about these things.

A Psalm of His Coming

The Lord is mighty. The Lord is merciful and instructs us in knowledge and wisdom. He calls to His creatures to return and change their life. He attempts to save them from their own foolishness. The Lord is mighty in battle and ever victorious. He roars from on high, and the whole earth trembles.

Who is like the Lord God? He makes His rain come down and scatters His lightning and thunder. He saves His judgment for the wicked but will spare those who are righteous in the land. Who can you compare to the Lord God? The idols of man tremble and fall on their faces before Him.

Worship the God of Holiness and hold Him as sacred. Come into His presence with singing and give thanks to His Name. He destroys the pride of the haughty and lifts up the head of the weak. He despises the proud in their conceit, but to the simple He shows wisdom. Who does man think he is to set himself up in the place of God, acting as if he is wise enough to teach when he knows nothing of God as He really is? God will blow him away like dust and like the small dust before a whirlwind, he will be carried away and forgotten forever. Amen.

The Lord God is mighty. He restores the souls of His Saints and keeps them safe in all troubles. He gives them peace in the midst of chaos and food in times when all are hungry. Blessed Be His Name. There is none like our God. Amen. Let the Heavens praise His Name, for He is merciful, just and true; and His mercy endures forever.

The Lord does not respect the proud or the rich. He has no regard for big bank accounts. However, He respects the "widow's mite" and the offering of the poor to Him. Their giving is from the heart and painfully given, therefore He holds the poor in high regards and remembers them, always listening for the prayer of the widow, the poor, and the orphan.

O praise His Name, you mighty Ones! The Lord remembers from generation to generation. He does not forget His Servants who have walked with Him nor their seed after them for all generations. He blesses them forever.

The haughty He curses, and the father's sins do follow in the children. Yet give thanks to the Lord for He does have mercy. If He had not left us a remnant, we would have been like Sodom and Gomorrah. He would take us away in our iniquities. But the Lord has long patience for the beloved fruit of the earth.

O listen all of you, whether your consciousness is high or low. *The Lord or Lady that lives within you is the only God and source of Life for you.* Listen within, and do what He or She tells you gladly, honoring God only and not men, and you will be led past death to eternal Life.

All you who are haughty and think you are special, remember Nimrod, who wanted to build a kingdom and a temple tall enough to reach God so he might be equal to Him and have a high-powered seat. Remember how God confounded him and took away all his followers in *one* hour. In *one* day all he sought to accomplish was gone. Listen to the lessons of history and know that the time is short for change.

The Mighty One is gearing up for the battle. The Lord of Hosts is His Name. He has lightning in His war chest and hurricanes and tornadoes. There is no way you can fight against Him when He makes the ground tremble under you. There is no way that your gunships can sail the seas to battle if He sends tidal waves upon you. Neither can you last very long if He causes immense snow or hail to fall upon you. Even if you batten down every hatch, you cannot endure nature's fury for very long or quickly recover when she sets her majestic forces against you.

In these ways, the land is recreated and the wealth of the rich is taken away and redistributed. Watch out, all you who have money and worship it as your savior. One day you'll warm your hands by the heat of its fire, trying to keep warm with it because you won't be able to buy a loaf of bread with it even though you're starving.

There is only ONE God, and He will confound the gods of men *and* those who worship them. Listen all you earthly gods, the Lord God will put you to shame. He will lift up the heads and souls that look to Him to be led by Him forevermore.

He has no regard for the proud, does not hear the prayers of the haughty, and only empties them. He causes disaster to pummel them so they will learn not to trust in their riches or worldly positions of power. He raises up those He chooses and casts down those who have not listened, which hardens some, as Pharaoh was.

Who is wise and mighty in wisdom like our God? Howl all you proud and rich ones, for the day of your destruction is near. And you who have robbed the lambs of the Lord, your God comes with a payback, for He has not been sleeping. Far from it. He has been awake and knows all your doings and secret thoughts. He will make them known, to your great embarrassment. Your glory and pomp will fail you. He will take away your great congregations and leave you with nothing but shame and disgrace, for He has declared, "Who shall annul My Words?"

Howl you shepherds of Christendom! Your end is coming, and your kingdoms, though mighty, will come down. Listen to the Lord your God and change, then you will be safe on the day of His anger and fierce wrath. The nations will tremble and separate. Many great cities will be thrown down. And who among you will be spared from His anger and wrath?

Blessed be the *meek* for they shall inherit the earth. Blessed be the *poor* for theirs is the Kingdom of Heaven. Blessed be the *pure in heart* for they shall see and rejoice in their God and the Light brought by His Mighty Arm. Blessed are the *peacemakers* for they shall be called *Sons and Daughters of God.* Blessed are *they who show mercy,* for God shall be merciful to them on the day when His wrath and justice poured out. Blessed are all *those who mourn as victims of wickedness,* for they shall be comforted. Blessed are *you who are reviled and persecuted when you speak for the Lord's sake.* He will save you on the day of man's anger and lift you up. Blessed are *they who when reviled, do not seek revenge.* God will get their revenge for them. He will surely repay their debt of kindness.

Listen, all you who think you are wise in earthly ways. You do not know the thinking of the Lord your God. He is not a man and does not think as a man. You have not known Him nor understood His ways. Therefore, surprise and terror will take you at the coming down of His Glorious Arm. Prepare yourselves because you cannot escape the justice of an offended God when He rises up.

April 21, 1996

Comfort My People

Let me comfort you, My People, in whose heart dwells My Law. Although you are Children and write like first-graders, I, the Teacher of My first-grade class, beam proudly at your efforts to obey Me. I certainly know what you are up against. And I see that you are trying. I will not judge you as seniors, for I know where each of you stands. I know what I have given you and the extent of your acceptance. I am starting slowly with you so that our lessons intensify a little at a time; that way you may all learn and grow together, even if not equally.

For some of you, My presence in the forefront of your minds and hearts has advanced quickly so that pure lessons might be had. Regard Me kindly for this pre-instructive gift, for I will be able to teach you purely and rightly. You will not be taught by haughtiness or violence. I will give you direction and foundation levels one by one, that you may build up a strong house in Me and literally become My New Jerusalem Church.

So receive your lessons as first-graders, and do not be ashamed of your efforts. My teachings are not like man's, and you do not need to be afraid of ridicule from your peers. Instead, love one another and grow together, for this is My will for you. You are all like sheep needing My guidance and direction.

What is Growth?

What is *growth in Spirit* as you move through the steps and levels of maturity? It is solid, stable thinking…the cessation of doubt and wishy-washy attitudes about what you believe…peace and calm within, instead of turmoil. Growing into maturity means keeping your eye, your heart, and your mind on Me at all times. It means no more double-mindedness.[78] This can be brought about by ceasing to hear all other teachers and allowing yourself to be taught by only ONE. The opinions of others will only confuse you because they are all saying something different. They all point in different directions, saying "Do this!" or "Don't do that!"

As your Commander, I tell you *Look only to ME*, like little children needing to be fed. As you come to ME alone, diligently, you will be fed by Me. I am the SOLID ROCK upon which My True Church is founded and not upon creeds or dogmas. Believing a thing is true does NOT make it real in you. I AM THE REAL THING that

---

[78] See James 1:2-12 for a discussion of seeing your trials as a privilege and keeping your mind unwavering in its focus on God.

must be introduced and then embraced before anyone can truly believe that *I Am*.

When have you had the courage to believe, except in fables, myth, and superstition? The foundation in which you have believed shakes and trembles under the weight of My words. This should be evidence to you that it is sandy. I AM THE ROCK AND UPON ME I WILL BUILD MY CHURCH. It will not tremble and give way but will remain strong in you. By My words, I am building My strong foundation in you. By levels and degrees, through My teaching and that of the Holy Spirit, this will be accomplished.

Do My words reach into your soul and burn there? Do they seem solid enough to stand on? Indeed, My words will stand forever. They do their own work, which is eternal. You are all weak through man's theology. I challenge you to take what you have learned to accept as doctrine and all your good ideas and replace them with My foundation of truth as I feed it to you. For man has nothing to do with what I give, except to write it for Me. These things are no less inspired by the Holy Spirit than your beloved scriptures that you cherish. I am the Lord that gave them through you, and I am willing and able to give you more and to restore those teachings lost to you through the hands of those who sought to destroy My Name while building their own kingdom.

O foolish man who thought to change and destroy My records! How dare you spite the Living God! I know all your deeds. As the very hairs of your heads are numbered, so are your secret thoughts. I have come to teach those that seek it how to stand on a firm foundation.

However, understand that I will not let you eat from My table *and* from the table of men, for one will ruin the other. If you have your eye on man's things and ideas, if you will not let go of them and continue to hang on to the old ideas, you will remain confused. I call for a COMPLETE SEPARATION if you want to be My Servant. Do you think I will allow you to be as Judas was, a member of My camp and of My enemy's camp as well? Only if I want another Judas experience, which I do not.

Seek Me all you ends of the earth, and turn away from your wicked ways among men. Why would you want to die?

O wicked house of Christendom, you serve Me with your mouths, yet in your hearts you are servants to idols and corruption. The roof man has built over your heads with his doctrine and theology is about to fall on you, and I ask you, are you willing to flee from this?

You that have a human form and listen to radio preachers or TV preachers must understand that they, too, seek to yoke you to them. They want to make members of those who can't or won't attend churches so they can take tithes from you. Do you know that tying yourself to them in membership only means you will help them pull their heavy financial load? Do you see a yearly financial record of how those funds are spent…or if those funds are taxed? Is there any accountability? Do you know what you are really giving to or how little of it is used for My purpose? No. You cannot know. You are giving to men, so how can I bless you?

You "give to get," and I cannot bless such giving. Watch, I will blow upon it and it will be gone. For the sake of the souls of the rich I take it away that they will not trust in it. In the time of calamity, they will bow to their god of money saying "Save me!" but the money will be worthless for buying food. Then they will turn and cry to Me. But I will not hear them simply because they spent their time in the days of preparation clinging to their own gods.

O man, do not linger in your mortality. Stay no longer in your ignorance. With My words comes responsibility, and you, having been warned, will be left without excuse.

Blame it on whomever you like, but in the end you will have to deal with ME. With all your secret sins you will be without a place to hide, for I am the ONLY safe place. I am the ONLY shield and buckler you have to trust. And I am the ONLY Redeemer who can truly save you from yourself and thus My Judgment.

Hear Me, My People, the Lord God is ONE LORD! Whoever claims to teach Me must submit to My Authority. When I send greater ones than those you have clung to and listened to, even they must put the worldly self aside to listen and learn or be destroyed. So cling to that which is REAL AND TRUE. If you want the PURE TRUTH then you must receive it from the PURE SOURCE, otherwise it will be a mixture of half-truths and half-lies, which is no better than what you have always known, with no delivering power.

My shepherds should jump at the chance to see My teachings unveiled before them. Yet they do not. Why? Because it threatens their theology and the dogma they have embraced and taught. It exposes them as wrong and way off My Foundation of Truth, like *all* men. It threatens their seat and position of power, their esteem from other men, and their profit. Therefore they are angered. In My own days upon the earth, I also challenged the established authority, and they certainly did buck and roar and shout "Heresy!" Finally, they crucified Me in an effort to keep their power, place, and nation.

Beware, Children, of robbers and thieves. Separate yourselves from them and cease to be captives caught in their delusion. The time will come when I will show who truly speaks for Me and who does not, for I am the Christ, Amen.

Living Epistles

Awaken to Me, My Little Ones. Do you see My Light coming forth in all the darkness that surrounds you? It is bursting forth like a *Sonrise*. Wipe the slumber from your eyes and behold Me with praise and thanks, for I, your Redeemer, will return your praise to you and give you My Joy.

My still, small voice calls many to hear Me, but few indeed are there who listen to know My Truth or WHO I AM. So few see My wisdom. I wish they would become *Living Epistles* and witnesses for the highest consciousness.

I long for your complete and full maturity. Today My Grace is like a lifeline thrown to a drowning man, one who is being tossed to and fro by the billowing waves of the tempest and cannot do anything to rescue himself as the storm continues to rage around him. I, your Redeemer, can calm the waters of your distress and remove the clouds of your discontent. I can give you joy, everlasting joy, to replace your displeasure, but first you must learn praise. Praise Me when you are happy. Praise Me when you are sad. Praise Me in the good times, but especially when times are bad.

Let your light shine so that men will be drawn to your unusual way of managing yourself. Let your testimony – humble and contrite – be offered continually to men as a pathway to guide all to My Love *for* you and My Love *through* you. Let your daily walk be in constant communion with Me. Only by doing so can I direct you to people and places where I can use you according to My purposes and plans. Do not let your life be caught and cast away by the things of this world. Do you know that through Me, by Grace's redemption, you are citizens and ambassadors of the Kingdom of Heaven, and are merely strangers and pilgrims walking here in these strange lands?[79]

Illuminate the darkness with rays of *Sonshine* found only by practicing the consciousness of heaven. Seek to add to the peace, the love, and the glory of God. Do not detract from the glory of God by being disobedient in front of others. If they see you, a child of God who does not obey, then neither will they. Remember, spiritual DNA

---

[79] Read Hebrews 11 for its inspired teaching about faith and recognizing that those who describe themselves as *nomads* and *strangers* "make it plain that they are in search of their real homeland," which is not the country they came from, but their home in heaven.

– spirituality that you *Do Not Apply* – is a blight on your souls and a poison to all, saved or unsaved, who witness it in your daily life.

Work to demonstrate the fruits of My Holy Spirit. What good will it do for you to speak in tongues, heal the sick, or offer words of wisdom and knowledge if your vessel is not polished with all the fruits mentioned by Paul? There is little profit for your Redeemer. Be like a tree that bears twelve kinds of fruit, and men will see My Truth and will be drawn by their hunger to feed at My Table. I say to all who hear My words, "Come to Me and I will fill you with My richness. In these last days, let Me make you Living Epistles of My New Jerusalem Church."

Come and let Me give you My Faith. Even though the Sons and Daughters of men seek Me wholeheartedly, it is like trying to pull water from an underground cistern in a desert using an old rusty hand pump. Much time and effort is required to draw. Too often, only a cup of water is drawn which has to satisfy the thirst of many and must be protected so that it will not be spilled before they can use it.

However, the Sons of God will be like Niagara Falls, pouring themselves from the high into the low places with torrents beyond measure that satisfy thirsty multitudes. They will pour out living waters beyond measure, and I, the Redeemer, will fill them daily without any effort on their part. Come to Me *early in the day* so I can fill you with My Faith, My Love, My Hope, My Joy, My Righteousness, and My Truth. You, Sons and Daughters of God, will be My Living Epistles to all.

Come to Me that I may come to you. Let Me sprinkle you with My grace abundantly. Let Me teach you the true value of forgiveness. As I have shown you forgiveness, in an even greater measure will you demonstrate its principle to the sons of men.

Remember always, *the unforgiving are unforgiven.* This is a benchmark principle upon which I will continue to build within and through you. Forgive the trespass. Forgive yourself so that you may progress beyond what hindered you. Do not let anger or vengeance become mud in your conduit. Do not constantly remind yourself of the insults, frustrations, and angers of the world. Leave all memories of these behind. Put them at the foot of My Cross and allow Me to bless them, making something beautiful from all your failings and those of your brother. Do it so that everyone may be forgiven. By honoring these commandments with purity of heart, the sons of men will learn to see the pattern of their Redeemer, and I will instruct you in how to be Sons of God who enjoy the fullness and maturity necessary to become My Living Epistles.

An Essay on Writing

A necessary prerequisite to writing is understanding this: Garbage going in results in garbage coming out. Out of the treasure chest of a man's heart comes his words. In this way, his true thoughts, his feelings, his gods, his loves, are made manifest.

Assess yourselves. What is the thing you like to talk about the most? Is it a hobby, or a notion, or a cause? Are you always trying to sell something? What "master" do you serve within?

To write clearly and hear clearly you must come to know inner stillness. You cannot be constantly filling your heads with noise of any kind. Nor can you be filled by books and tapes, or you will *parrot* what you have heard. My words of prophecy become pure only after all these influences have stopped. Even your own thoughts must cease regarding what I am saying, otherwise they will pollute My words.

Listen quietly, Children, and wait until I bring forth an impetus or an urge from within you that is forceful in its direction and unlike anything you have known. The way, manner, and purpose of the Living God is like a freight train speeding out of the control of the conductor. But do not be afraid, for *I Am* in control. To you who would try to derail My purpose, it would feel out of control.

I have a Kingdom to build and one to destroy, and only through My wisdom must this be done. The thinking or good planning of no man will suffice for the Holy Spirit's direction on any man's part. Therefore attune yourself to Me, and do not think you can challenge My authority or do things your own way. Insubordinates will be moved off to the side of the battlefield until they learn not to rebel against My orders.

Which one of you can even glimpse My battle plan? And who is the general among men who can challenge Me? There are none. So seek to submit yourself to Me. Be humble before Me and seek My directing influence, for only in oneness will we have victory. If you are off fighting your own private war, you are no help to Me. Instead you become a potential enemy. Beware then, all you with your own ideas, that you are A.W.O.L. – absent without leave – from My battalions.

Peace can only be found in the absence of self-will that tries to depend on its own strength. I lend My strength to the weak and point My Sword at the proud. I choose the small who do not think so much of themselves and scorn those who are full of themselves and their own wisdom.

My directions are pointed and My foundations being revealed are like nothing you have ever seen or heard before. Thus, how can you possibly help Me from your own wisdom? Can you bring My lost teachings from long ago to your fellow man? I say no. And tragically, the scrolls and writings being found by archaeologists and excavators are being hurriedly bought up and stuffed away by the Church so that you will never see the good parts of them, lest you discover they are vultures, snakes, and sordid people.

O Children, do not let your lives dangle in the hands of men who care nothing for you. It is with ME that you will have to deal on the day of judgment. Surely you cannot blame "so and so" for not teaching you right when you had a bible of your own and could also read, pray, and seek My face on your own. You, yourself, could have made the decision to follow Me.

Listen to My words... I AM COME to draw to Me whoever will come to Me, whoever will obey and humble themselves. I will raise their consciousness and save them in the Kingdom of My Father. They will not receive the mark of the Beast, for certain destruction awaits those men who believe in the world.

I Need You

The Lord welcomes you to His fold and thanks His Father for the wisdom that brought you here. Your life is not your own to the degree you have given it to Me. I need you to write for Me and to use the gifts, the *jewels* I have laid within you, to benefit My flocks.

Therefore, My need for you is great and intense. Never think that I do not appreciate you. Some who think they do not need Me scoff at Me. They turn up their noses. Others may reject My manifestation through you. But it is *with ME* they will have to deal, and it will not go well with them on the day of My repayment.

Keep My marks about you and in you, the marks of Christ. Persecution comes for the word's sake and indeed it will be so. Understand that even as your Master suffered, so will you. To know My suffering leads to knowing My glory, and we will share it together. Let vindication be Mine, for I alone can see and judge righteously. You *pray* for your enemies and *forgive them*, just as I did for My Father's sake. That way you will be free of their blood.

The hand of man who follows Me cannot be stained with the blood of getting his own revenge or he will suffer with the guilty on My judgment day.

We Need Each Other

Good morning, My Little flock. What a great day it will be for the Sons of Mine, Sons after My own heart. If only I could convey to each of you the depth of My Love for you and the breadth of My hope for you as you continue to climb higher and higher to My Holy Truths.

Each day I long to reveal to each of you a special teaching, a special word, and a special blessing of your own, that it might ignite your flame of hope and understanding of everlasting life, a life in which our communion will reveal new and precious revelations to My other Sons. What is possible is a love where all can share in joy and rejoice in Me. New lessons can be taught through My impressions upon you, and you can then share this with the others with the purpose of helping all. Everyone can move into the fullness of maturity filled with gladness and peace.

I see a Body where all come to know and equally respect the other parts of the Body, rejoicing in the good working of one another. I will direct you as you move onward, with singleness of purpose, towards the utmost of My Kingdom, every step allowing a new vision which builds upon yesterday's vision and restores joy upon joy at each new revealing.

How would it be if the eyes were captured by one sight and wanted to remain in that place while the ears were being called to a distant song far beyond that view? Shall the eyes make the ears wait before exploring the call? I say no. My Body will go where I direct, as quickly or as leisurely as I say. I know when the feet must rest and the belly must be fed, and I take all into consideration when deciding what is best for all.

Sons and Daughters of Mine, know that I regard each of you as necessary for the fulfillment of all, for the growth of all. What good is a hand with no fingers? How can it feed the mouth or lift the Body when it climbs? You can see that, because of the disability, the rest of the Body would be cheated and deprived of My good intentions to accomplish My purposes and plans for the entire Body.

Look deep into yourself and at your sisters and brothers, and rejoice together in Me with a newfound appreciation for what I give you. Let it be a benefit to all as our Body continues along the journey from glory to glory.

Know Contentment Anywhere

See Me in all things so that what it means to step into the Christ will be seen and understood. The *I Am* is both great and small and delights in being everywhere. It can be found dwelling from the heights to the lowest places. From each place *I Am* instructs and seeks to teach you blessed lessons from My heart. All are necessary for your experience, and from each place I attempt to impart kernels of My Truth so that you might see and understand the beauty of both the heights and the lows, and the Light that is in both the great and the small. When the Sons of God come to the fullness of that understanding and experience the Christ within, then My wisdom can truly impart a peaceful contentment wherever they might be found, and joy will forever fill their hearts.

Sons and Daughters of Mine, I, your Redeemer, will raise you or lower you to where you can be of most value to My purpose and/or My plan. I will fill you or empty you as the journey demands so that our work can be done completely. By doing so, we can help and save your brother man. Know that I am with you wherever you might be, high or low, great or small, and be at peace so that My grace might flow abundantly. By so doing, you will have great results and this will encourage you.

Yes, Sons and Daughters, give the vessel of your life fully to Me and allow Me to be your only Guide. I know all the trails throughout the valley or along the cliffs that we must transcend to find the lost one and return him to My fold.

Clear your minds of all your preconceived notions of how things should be. Clear your mind until you are a blank slate and able to focus solely on Me. I, alone, can guide you to the blessings I have ordained for you.

I will show you the radiant Light of each vision along the way. Surrender your vision and release your hearing that you might see what I see, hear what I hear, and feel the goodness of all I feel. In so doing, we can truly become as one; and I, your Redeemer, can manifest you as a "Son."

My Light will be your Light, My Love will be your Love, My words will be your words, and My ways and paths will be your ways and paths. IN UNITY AND PURITY we will forevermore be ONE.

Come with Me. Yes, Come. Come. Come. Let us go now, for our journey has only begun. Higher! Higher! Higher! Let us be a delight to our Father's Throne and be thankful for eternity to be called and chosen as His own. Amen. ◆

April 21, 1996

The Race to the Finish Line

Find ways to use the gifts I have given you. Look for ways to benefit the group in which I have placed you. Do not fear that you will fail to hear Me clearly, for you *will* make mistakes sometimes. That's why I gave you *My eraser of Love and My ruler of Patience,* so you could endure and learn and grow.

My Children, I have no chalkboard, but I do have pads and pens for you to write My lessons on so you can study them. Testing will be on an *individual* basis to measure your growth. You will see for yourself how well you stand or fall in them. My testing is in the daily situations and unexpected circumstances of your lives, and that is the only way to really know how you are doing. Who is the haughty one, thinking he or she is above the other students? I will be quick to depose anyone who gets up on their self-made pedestal.

We will have order in our group, and you will treat one another as I treat you, with loving kindness and not strictness. Remember that there is a time for play, a time for learning, and also a time to "gab" with one another. I am as *serious* a Teacher now as I was while on the earth and so are My lessons. Therefore, behave yourselves, My Little Ones, and pay attention to Me.

Even though you do not see Me, I am among you, observing your order and willingness to learn, as well as how much you are willing to allow yourselves to be used. Set aside any attempts to prove yourselves, for this kind of motivation comes from your will, not Mine. Seek only to receive My words and impressions in complete humility, and do not cringe to write them or share them. Each of you has a gift to share that others will benefit from, not just yourself. Thus, do not hide the talent I gave you for that would be selfishness and fear.

My life lessons must be learned, and you are all literate children. Therefore be willing to learn. Be willing to write. Be willing to receive. Know that My secretary has been pre-trained and will help you as much as she can after meetings are over. In the meantime, listen to Me carefully and intently in the midst of your lessons. Do not let your thoughts fly away to something you need to do or think about later, for this blocks the path of your receptivity to My Voice.

You do not know that My Plan and Purpose is to publish your first grade work in My newsletter nationwide. The very idea scares you, but many are still in kindergarten and need your lessons – which will seem advanced to them – so that they, too, can have hope of attaining Christ-consciousness. This is how I will do My work among you and among the people of My Nation. You do not need to know or understand every detail of My doings. You must simply write the sentences I give you and do your best for Me. Afterwards, it is up to Me to bless the understanding of others, for you do not know what they need.

In preparation, I ask you to be aware of what you put into your heads and hearts, for this is what feeds your minds. A lot of mud will only cause a clogged path of receptivity and result in a lessening of My ability to teach you.

I also ask that you refrain from studying and listening to the teachings of men, whether by words, books, or tapes, for this will influence your thinking during the times you try to write for Me. If you were only writing to your own self, it wouldn't be such an interference, but what I have in mind is to teach others through your experience, thus I would like that experience to be as pure and clean as possible. Since you are responsible to Me to get it right for their sakes, I ask you to free yourselves of the influence – the leaven of the

Pharisees – so you may pass out My unleavened Bread to the joy of all.

The Oak and The Evergreen

The treasures of our God's wisdom are great, and greater yet is the illumination of His Risen Son, our Redeemer, to His faithful and chosen ones. Because of the Lord, we can learn to elevate ourselves to the Source from which pure wisdom flows.

He knows whether we need a deluge to wash away our stains or only a sprinkle to nourish the heart's garden where His treasured plants of truth are maintained. The wisdom from on high is very great, greater than man could know. The sons of men treasure words handed down to them from the past. They seek old knowledge and fall in love with feelings that lead to bondage and can never last.

The sons of men, wise as they might be, can be likened to an oak tree. It rises from its root planted deep within the soil and spreads its limbs and branches in a fashion that draws our attention downward. The mighty oak is the hardest, the most stubborn and unyielding tree, relying only on itself. But if it cannot bend when the storms of change are in the air, My high winds break it easily. It will be left shattered, a casualty of the storm, whose fate is to be cut up and carried away. Like man's knowledge, the mighty oak spreads its leaves for only a season until the cold winds blow. Then the leaves turn color and men are drawn to look at their beauty until the leaves are left lifeless and their knowledge drops away, to be spread like colorful papers upon the lawn. Now they are a nuisance as the autumn breeze blows their knowledge about, dry and brittle, crumbling everywhere and needing to be swept away. Then look at the mighty oak tree. See it naked in the snow, and ask yourself "Where did man's knowledge – its leaves – go?" This is the way it has been for the sons of men forever and a day. Yes, all of them and their wisdom have blown away.

Now see the Sons of God and liken them to the evergreen. Now their life continues throughout eternity, and their knowledge is everlasting and endures through the ages. They are soft and have learned to bend, even bowing to the ground when stormy winds blow. When the storm is past, they remain pointing toward the highest, showing the way toward heaven where true wisdom can be found. They know that God grants them words beyond that which they could come up with themselves, and these words bring Light. Thus they humbly speak and work in joy, health, and peace. They continuously point to heaven's Throne and give everlasting praise to the Father and to His Risen Son.

April 21, 1996

Freedom from Despair

When you see the beginnings of wisdom, you also see the fear of the Most High, which is not really fear as much as deep respect. If you have respect for My teachings, words, and sayings, then you'll not be so quick to cast them aside to do what you want. If you have respect for My feelings, you will not cast My Love behind your back and seek other Lovers or Teachers.

When you grasp the Truth of God within you, you will be delivered from the chains of the captivity of your present minds! The limitations taught to you by man's teachings and laws will be BLOWN AWAY, and the freedom and joy you once lived in when you really knew Me will be yours again. The grandeur of these new possibilities, new vistas, and panoramas beckons you to see what I am telling you.

In this joyous rebirth there will be a new freedom from the routines religion has taught you. *Never forget* – anything which does not come spontaneously from you will create a dark sense of duty, drudgery, and loathing!

Your praise must come from *love* for Me. Your happiness must not be a mask worn for certain occasions then removed in private. Offer Me all of your darkness, and My Light will set you free from your prison of despair. Much of this despair is caused by lack of confidence or seeing one's self as less than you think you should be.

O Little Children, consider those of you who follow Me to be children of the King. Even if you think you have nothing, you possess all knowledge and wisdom because of your access to Me! And what could be better than this? Do you seek to know? Do you seek to understand? I will give you lessons individually, teaching you *privately* if given the chance. So, diligent Ones, do your lessons and seek Me for sentences to put on your paper, for I have much to write, and one or a few cannot do it. Therefore seek to apply yourself.

Flowers in My Garden of Joy

From the depths of willingness I burst forth as a flower in bloom upon your heads, My Little Precious Plants. You may be unaware of your beauty, as well as your function in My garden, but know that you are a joy to Me. As the Gardener, I have planted you in My garden wherever I thought best, that I may have just the right harmony of color and size among My plants. Do not worry or wonder if your perfume is right or if any other is better. Concentrate only on *being* and lending your joy and beauty to the entire place.

I want no weeds in My garden of joy. Yet thoughts, as weeds, overrun My whole garden, destroying, trampling, and sowing seeds of destruction. Therefore, do not let weeds begin to overtake you as you sit in My classroom. Your thoughts disrupt the harmony of the place and destroy the unity and song of all My flowers. Joy and peace would be usurped and then look what a mess we would have.

My Children, I have set you all together in My Garden that you might see and know PURITY AND KINDNESS and become a perfect reflection of them. Let these qualities glow within you and allow your great radiance to shine throughout the garden. Let nothing disrupt My class. I put no substitute teacher in charge.

Yet know that I need helpers above your level so you will see it is possible to achieve the consciousness I am teaching. If you have no example, you might give up in defeat. I am one example – and was once human just like you. *Go after that holy prize*, I say to you. Commit yourself to the highest level of consciousness by remaining obedient to the direction coming from the Spirit of Christ within you.

Hearing Lessons

My messages flow quickly and furiously through those who are able to receive them and whose ears are tuned to Me. I have work to do, My Children, and you are helping to further My work.

Circumcise your ears and listen only to Me. The time of "hearing lessons" is now. The time of wide open prophecy against Christendom is coming. Receive your lessons with all due diligence, for the time of open vision is not far from you. If you are struggling with doubt over My words at THAT TIME, you will not be able to give My message of great importance to My People.

Again, your diligence is *most important*, and your individual tutoring sessions with Me most required, if you will be speakers with Me in the battle ahead.

The Jealous Shepherd

Pay attention, all you who follow Me and know that I am a Jealous Shepherd when it comes to the safety and protection of My flocks. If wolves come near My flocks, I get angry and raise My Staff against them. But if you allow them access to you of your own free will, I must relinquish you to their care, no matter how much I am offended at this.

I am preparing each of you to be shepherds for Me, and no matter how unworthy My shepherds may be or what I know of you inwardly that you DO NOT know, I must give you the right to choose. But you should know My grief over this! It says that you did not see Me as a worthy Trainer, or sought more or better than I gave you, or that you were captivated by a good speaker from the world.

O Little Ones, *tantalizing* are the sermons of men, yet they are only *husks*; they are *not Life*. Therefore, I require you to choose and not attempt to believe you can serve both, for in so doing you serve neither and only delude yourself.

My Kingdom is Coming

O Churches! O Temples! O Sarkieus! Beware! I am coming to ruin your walls and foundations. They are built on sand, on men's wisdoms.

Watch, My People, and you will see My Kingdom is coming. Open your hearts for My calling. Come, O come to Me, you who can hear me. Leave everything. Come now before the temple collapses. I warn you.

Come, My People, and rejoice at your Father's side. The New Earth is welcoming all you who want to come.

To My flocks I say, "Be aware that I have come to lift your mind, to raise your consciousness up to the highest places so you can see My Kingdom. Separate yourselves from your old ways, habits, and beliefs for My sake. Those who listen and obey My words will be blessed by My rewards. Those who devote their lives to Christ-consciousness will share in eternal Life. I bless those who are willing to bend their will to the will of the Father and serve his ways of Love, Joy, and Truth.

To The Battle

The work ahead is serious work and the battle a serious battle in which there will be many casualties. Therefore you will need to lay foundations of solid strength in yourselves so that you will be able to stand when the time comes. My Armor of protection is not yet within or around you. But do not be afraid. In your nakedness I will clothe you at the right moment and give you the armor you need for the battle. Do not seek to do this yourself, for you only know how to apply mud to yourselves. Mud is a plaything for children. Therefore, wash yourselves from the mud of the past and let My cleansing Truth flow over and through you. My torrents of *Truth will wash and regenerate you*.

I need you to grow up in Me, to grow into My fullness. You have not known what this means; however, it means you will be *soldiers for Me* and will take a stand for Love, Joy, Patience, Liberation, and the Right Use of all things. For these, I will armor you. I am your Shield of Faith and Love, your Uniform of Joy and Patience, your Helmet of Liberation, your Breastplate of Right-use-ness.

These will not be applied by yourself as you see fit – God forbid! – but spontaneously, as they are given to you, always as MY GIFT.

The Sword in your hand will be My words of prophetic utterance, and you must learn how to wield it. Understand that it is very sharp, yet is motivated only by My Spirit. Indeed, put My Gospel of Peace shoes on your feet or you will walk naked and barefoot to the shame of all.

I have horses on which you will ride and wings on which you will fly. These are *prayer* and *intercession*.[80] With a pure and humble

---

[80] *Intercession* comes from the word "intercede" and means "to mediate, or to step in between conflicting parties in order to help settle things." As it is used here, it refers to the need for us to step in and help one another. Also, when someone is struggling with a poor attitude toward others, with ill

attitude and in union with your Maker, your words or requests will be shaped by Me, and if you say only what I have given you to say, we will have the victory. Your will cannot be involved – only Mine. When we are in complete alignment, My words are given to all those who seek them. If it is yourself who needs the help, then be aware that to hear what I tell you, and *do* it, is *Life* to you. To hear it and refuse it is *suicide*. This is how all My battles go, and the casualties are many. Only through willingness on their part can the enemy be won, but even if they choose suicide, they cannot touch you.

Front Line Warriors

The fierceness of the battle is not experienced by most of the army, but the *front line* receives the most wounding. You may ask, "Who is greater… those on the front line of the battle? Or those in successive lines behind them who seem to be under My protection?"

I say, do not be distracted with questions about who is greater. My front line of defense will need to be uplifted. They will need the intercessions of the others or else they cannot long endure, no matter how steadfast.

My witnesses are pinpoint places of firing. They draw the battle upon themselves while My Sons go around this to assault the fortress of Christendom. You marvel at their strength. Yet do you know that they are *vulnerable* without the strength of your intercessions?

Listen, all My front-line leaders whom I have set up, there will be *intense focuses of attack*. Therefore, build walls of prayer around My instruments that they may be protected. Otherwise they

---

health, or loss of a job, etc. you may be the one who says just what they need to hear and your words may make a huge difference in how they think, feel, or act – but you must say these words only when prompted by the Christ-consciousness within. These words appear spontaneously and are free of judgment.

will die because of *your* lack of strength as they lay wounded upon the battlefield, bleeding as if unnoticed.

My war will get hotter with every newsletter published. The focal point of fire will be the writers who bring forth My words of power and authority to break down Christendom's fortress of strength so that you might go on in to possess the city. Pay attention, My Servants in mighty prayer, for the battle is not just for those on the front line to bear, nor the wounding, but is yours as well.

You Who Forget God

All of you who forget God to follow your own direction will not make much progress, or keep what progress you do make. Neither will you have success in the end, even though you fight hard for it, going so far as to murder your brothers and sisters to obtain it at any cost.

You who seek to save your ministry or seats of power and wealth as My Truth comes forth – beware! I will expose you before all. They will see you are a fraud.

Woe to you who wound the lambs who write for Me because you do not like My words. Those words will burn you as if they were fire and curse you at your end. I don't care *what* your reasoning or motivation is, how good your purpose may seem to you, or how righteous. You will be destroyed for taking a destructive posture against My Little Ones, for I Am the Repayer.

April 22, 1996

A Song of Battle

Awake and arise, all you soldiers of the King, and prepare yourselves for battle. Send the Rangers out, My special forces, and prepare to receive My Commands. Listen! Listen, O My Sons, for the battle cry. Sound the trumpets to alarm the nations of Christendom to prepare their warrior chieftain. Watch and remain aware! The battle rages hot. Pay attention or you will fall, for in the hidden places where Satan has hold of you, you will fall upon his sword.

My Little Ones, keep My banner raised in front of you. Keep it raised and flying high. Do not stay in the kingdom of the dust, but use your wings and take to the sky. He that controls the air wins the battle. In the battle of the clouds, break free from every earthly chain. Stand up and proclaim My Name in victory and raise your consciousness high!

April 23, 1996

Horses and Chariots of Egypt

Every man has his own horse of doubt about Me. He gets on his horse and flees from My will until the day he finally accepts My truths. Then his horse of doubt becomes his strong companion. Look at the wisdom of God and the pure peace, trust, and love it teaches. Look at how this compares to the wisdom of men. The wisdom of men is based in fear, pride, ignorance, and illusion. Man's wisdom doubts My wisdom, and this doubt causes him to flee from Me until he can run no more. Then he must get down off his horse of doubt and confess to the Truth of My words.

Doubt is a plague on My people. Doubt pursues them like a strong enemy. The doctrines of men are like horses upon which men ride and in which they trust. Like chariots, these doctrines carry men forward blindly, pulled by a team of horses of doubt, when their Father is waiting to embrace them graciously. Like the men of old who sought help from Egypt because they had swift horses and chariots, today's men will be disappointed. They will all be overthrown. Woe to those who turn to Egypt and desire to stay on horses and trust in their chariots.

To C.W... By Faith, Not Sight

The power of the Christ in Jesus speaks to you in order to bring you the courage to write holy words of instruction without fear or doubt, regardless of what others think, and without concern for whether the people dear to you are mature enough to receive such revelations.

Every man and woman will receive My revelations to his or her own capacity to believe, and there is nothing you can do about the rest. You are the pen in My hand, not the interpreter of My words. You can help shape things in some categories, but in others you cannot, for in some things they will not believe no matter what you tell them or show them. This lack of belief is not directed towards you but towards *Me*, and I have and will openly address it.

Therefore, listen, My Children, and understand that what I give you to write is *new*, even to you. I do not give you the responsibility of being teachers who understand the principles that govern the holy. I give them to you so they might be *received deeply* by you and shared with others. You are not to add to them or subtract from them using your own understanding.

Rather, let each receive and believe according to his own capability and measure. Each one's willingness to let go of the old, the loved, and the coveted will set the measure of his ability to receive My New.

By no means can you find the basis to support the new on your own. You must receive it BY FAITH, trusting Me to reveal more concerning it. I know what I am doing and in what measure to collapse the old.

I will reign over the New in all those who are willing to receive it, even though many are too young or too afraid to receive the strong meat I bring forth. They begin to cry as their house of cards falls. Even so, I will continue to destroy it, for it must be done. Even if they cry about it, it is good for them.

I bring forth Truth, and you are not to stand off from Me while you look for "proof." My revelation comes forth. To those who need proof at every step I say, "BY FAITH, NOT BY SIGHT will I pick and choose from among you. Those that willingly submit their entire basket of puzzle pieces will receive more than I take. Those who withhold anything from Me will find their whole basket turned upside down on the floor."

Whoever has ears to hear, let him hear what Spirit says to the Church. And let him heed the instruction of the Almighty, who knows better than he what the Truth is. Do not trust in the knowledge that man has taught you. Let the knowledge you need be revealed by revelation. Otherwise you swim in a cesspool of religious knowledge that has no power to deliver. You will be *learning forever,* which you will think is good, *but you will never come to the knowledge of my Truth!* [81]

Again I say to you, "Look! I set forth a bowl of Bread. Will you accept it or reject it because it was not what you expected?" Listen carefully, for I am warning you that My teachings and revelations are not like man's. I will destroy and replace man's teachings in all of you who are willing to believe Me. For I am, indeed, the very Truth, Jesus Christ is My Name. Amen.

Tree of Knowledge, Tree of Life

Woe to all of you who are not willing to receive revelation! The doctrine in your hand, to which you cling, will drown you in sorrow and doubt. Death will work in you and not Life. The fruit from the Tree of Knowledge tasted good and appealed to the sight of man and woman. They thought it was able to make them wise, so they ate it. The serpent said it would make them wise and like gods.

---

[81] See 2 Timothy 3:1-9 for a description of the dangers of the final days in a civilization that has lost contact with God.

I was the One who directed them *not* to eat it, for I knew that "death" would be the result, a veil would be drawn over their spiritual sight, they would remain distant from Me, and their doubt would cause disobedience to all My words. They would no longer be able to communicate with Me, we would no longer be close, and they would no longer worship My *Tree of Life*.

Certainly, they did not understand the *seriousness* of their choice, nor do you, My present day Children. Their choice was disobedience and unwillingness to eat that which was good.

Thus I now work to convince you that you can learn to see the Truth of My words. You who have long walked in the darkness of man's supposed "light," will you who have been blind now direct Me? Will you tell me that I – who am altogether Light – can't possibly be right because what I tell you is not according to My Bible?

Surely you must decide which master you will follow. The Author of *your* life stands begging to receive you and for you to receive Me. Yet you hold to a book, imperfectly written, which has had things taken out of it and other things added to it, you know not how or by whom. All this has been done so man might bring you under his dominion and force you to submit yourself to him who is no god, yet stands in the temple of God, showing off as if he were God. He is nothing but the son of perdition.[82]

I have told you that there would be a falling away and a time of great darkness because of this mystery of iniquity. I warned you that an anti-Christ would come who would stand against Me and My Truth. Now here we are at the end of days. I plead with you not to believe his poisonous doctrine anymore. It is a completely leavened bread of iniquity.

---

[82] See 2 Thessalonians 2:1-4

Receive My New teaching and work to understand it. Let the veil be removed from the eyes of all nations so that all might see the Light of My Coming. And remember – it is *to each of you I come.*

To whatever measure you receive Me you will see Me come. In whatever measure you receive My Truth, you will grow. And in your growth you will find the doctrine of the sons of perdition to be puke and vomit by comparison, and yourselves as dogs who keep returning to it.

It is time to grow up in Me, Children. I have put a great Light in you and those who believe and work to develop that Light will see the Christ in themselves and will come forth resurrected to real Life. Those who hold to the doctrine of lies and the great harlot will live in darkness and doubt.

Will you again reject Me and be ashamed of Me before all men? Would you again crucify the *Light of the World* because it wasn't what you expected? I hold out to you the Key of Life, the key that will unlock each of your prison doors. Your acceptance of My Key of Life is very important – by faith, not by *proof* – for proof is merely religious pride and flesh.

I hold out the fruit from the *Tree of Life,* and you are afraid of it because the fruit from the Tree of Knowledge is still in your hand. Drop that and come try a bite of My Fruit. You will see that with LOVE My fruit comes forth. And IN PATIENCE I extend it. You will *see and live in great Light* when you taste it. My goal is to *restore the unity and oneness of man with Me as it was at the beginning,* if only you will receive Me and once again become Sons of Light and not remain sons of men.

Climb down off your horses of doubt and do not take offense at My words. I am the Christ who died for you that I might demonstrate the Truth to you, cutting away the kingdom of flesh. Circumcise your heart to Me forever in the Kingdom of the Most High where I welcome you. Amen.

April 26, 1996

Angels of Light, Ministers of Unrighteousness

I, Jesus, your Redeemer, would have a word with all who think or wish to be recorded eternally in My Book of Life. You think that man's knowledge of the Holy Scriptures has been preserved and presented to your generations according to My Father's intent. You think His words have been rightly translated and set forth by your esteemed holy men, and that surely Christendom has and does tell My story in the manner I intended. You think your great schools of theological training and understanding have prepared missionaries to My liking. But I, your Redeemer, would have you know they are all poisoned cisterns fed by polluted streams for the benefit of Pharisees. They are all maintained by evil scribes, who for centuries have prevented, perverted, distorted, and disdained the purity of My Truth and the simplicity of My Grace, and all are without the facility to represent Me to My people.

Look for a minute at their results, yes even you ministers and missionaries of the status quo system. See My pattern from your elevated position. Before his transformation Paul was perhaps the greatest of the Pharisees. Yet I transformed him into a vessel more to My liking and more to My purpose. With him as My mouthpiece, I performed many miracles and edifying works in times much more perilous than those you face today. He did not have the provisions or tools available to you, My ministers and missionaries. He had manifested power. He brought glory to My mission and My Father's Throne, and he now lives and will be eternally recorded in earth *and* heaven as one of My own, because he allowed Me to work through him.

Where is your power? What miracles have you learned from your teachers at your great seminaries? Can you demonstrate it for Me or for the people over whom you presently preside? Can you heal them of their illnesses or do you only pray for them? Who do you pray to? The earth has not seen the manifestation of any results yet. Perhaps your lines of communication have been cut to My True Source of Power, healing, and Light. Maybe your great and grand professors robbed and deceived you... yet they still beckon you to come back for graduate seminars, promising that you will learn how to enhance your power or at least how to restore this power to you... and you flock like herds, dumb and blind, to your mentors.

Can't you see that they have no power? Nor do they understand the principles by which they might lay hold of My Power, yet they teach that which they know nothing about and charge you a fee to hear their dogmatic doctrines of emptiness. You leave their seminars more confused – and *without* that which you paid for. So the proverb is true: "The end state of that man is worse than the former." Meanwhile, My people perish for lack of Truth in your houses, O Christendom, and this is the way it has been from your beginning to your end. O ministers and missionaries of men's learning, can you not see that I, alone, can instruct and teach you My ways?

I, Jesus, your Redeemer, the One you profess to represent to your congregations and nations, do most emphatically declare to all with ears to hear that your text of My Father's word is a millstone around your necks.

All of My good and precious Truths that would give you the understanding you need to demonstrate the Truth for your flocks have been denied to you by men. Since you did not have the Truth of My Living Words, but were fed the half-truths of man's dead interpretations from centuries long gone, you could not know, nor are you responsible for, your downfall before Me at My Coming in these end days when I will work through My chosen vessels, My Living Epistles, yes, My manifested Sons of God, soon to be seen by all.

I am raising vessels to My liking. They will be like Paul, but with a double portion of My grace, My mercy, My Love and My clear and complete understanding of all things.

My new Pentecost will sweep the nations like a wildfire which you, Christendom, will not be able to extinguish, for it comes from Me and by Me. Neither Christendom nor any of her emissaries will be able to discount or distort the results. This new Pentecost and manifestation of My Sons of God will bring understanding and light to My Throne, the *I Am*.

Through My Risen Son of glory, Jesus the Christ, I will give them power from on high, power over the world below. Will your temples of death be able to compete with this? The *I Am* has declared that you, Christendom, present day Babylon, will fall and all your related governments, both of church and state, will learn to bow before Me, the Living God.

You will no longer twist My words to your advantage. Your alliances of church and state, subtle and hidden, will not offer you any support in these times to come, for *I Am* is a Living God. I will smash you into pieces, grind you into powder, and cast your remains to the wind, nevermore to be remembered in My New Earth Kingdom. Never again will you compromise My meaning, debate My words, or debase My Throne of Power in front of men.

The *I Am* has declared to you this day: the stench of your abominations has ascended to My heavenly realms, and the pollution of your secret alliances and unholy unions has descended to the foundations of all I have created. Now the *I Am* will clean My Creation and bring it to Me. Never again will *man* teach his brother about Me in the earth Kingdom. My anger is kindled against you, O Christendom, and you will not prevail against Me. I will swallow you up as I did Dathan and his followers and will begin anew with My pure Remnant, reserved for My risen Son, Jesus.

Come out of Sodom and Gomorrah all you inhabitants. It is not fit for beast or fowl, and surely not man. Come out of religious Babylon, for in an hour will I destroy her and all who stand and cling to her and her systems and her governments. I, your Redeemer, call to all with ears to hear. All of My sheep, hear Me and obey My voice.

The others will be left to the uncertainty of their own paths or that of their leaders. All kingdoms will bow and every tongue confess to Me, or be eternally left to their own damnation and destruction before our Father, the Almighty Creator of all. Amen.

Be Born of My Spirit

Come, be born of My Spirit, says your Lord. Experience My new birth. Be birthed into realms of joy. Be birthed into realms of power and delivered from sorrow and pain. Be born again in the essence of My Truth. Let Me handle the things and ways of the Spirit and see if I am indeed good meat, spiritual meat to your souls. You are starving for something *Real, something True.* The world has fed you worms by comparison and has poisoned your souls. Death is your end instead of *Life*.

You say you had Me once then lost the Essence of Life and the joy of your first experience? When Higher Consciousness began to fall, understand that death came riding in on the tail of man's rules and religious knowledge about Me. Death came about because you ate less and less of the Tree of Life, and more and more of the Tree of Knowledge. Finally drowning, you set up a false front and now your path is governed by dead religious routines. My joy has left you and you do not know where to turn.

Can you see a Light blazing before you? I am alive forevermore and I do away with the death and the darkness that has held you while you lay dormant and sleeping in your cocoon. Awaken! You will see that as you come to rebirth in Life and Spirit you have grown wings. Come! You are no longer a creature of the dust, for I have given you wings to soar above all your enemies.

Thus, *Come!* Let us soar together! My Truth will lead you to a place you do not know of. Nevertheless, you are itching to find out. But first stand still and let My warmth dry your wings and stretch them. You are not yet ready to jump into My new place. Let us live together for a while. Cast all that is behind you onto My Altar and let Me purify it and transform it into the fullness of My Truth. Man has given you husks, but I dawn in you like a glorious New Day. I sing you a song of deliverance from your captivity, a song of rejoicing.

All you who would like to follow Me must be willing to accept My Truth and reveal it to others as I direct you. Certainly these Truths will blast away the teachings of men and show them to be the dust of the earth. They will be recognized as sensual and devilish, coming from carnal mentality. You have received lies which have hurt you, but I am here to direct you out of your bondage. Whosoever has an ear to hear and eye to see, along with a desire to be freed from your chains of drudgery and defeat, will be released from captivity.

Listen To the Voice of Your Almighty Deliverer!

No man can teach as I can. Listen to me and your soul will live. I will manifest Myself to you.[83] What you have learned is *darkness and the shadow of death.* But come, O Come to the Light of My consciousness for I desire that Light for you.

I come to those that truly seek Me. I wait patiently for those who are satisfied with their religious commitment to get tired of such foolishness so that I can show them True Peace, True Light, and wonders beyond their belief.

My sheep, let Me separate you from the goats. By your heart's desire to follow Me I will know which way you go. I will expose all that is false, all that is phony and fake in your midst. Those who love darkness and don't want the hideous, naked truth about Christendom to be seen for what it really is will be vehemently angry.

---

[83] See John 14:21 for the promise made to us if we align with the will of the Father.

Christendom declares herself rich, blessed, and has enjoyed great increases from My people's goods. She says she is in need of nothing. Yet she does not know that she is blind and miserable and naked and wretched.

Listen to me, you sheep in My pasture! There is a gate out of Christendom that is quickly closing. I bid you, come out and do not enter it again. The battle lines are drawn in the Spirit and you do not know where to be safe.

I say, "Come into your private prayer closets and seek Me. Do not go back to the ministers who claim to know Me for your money's sake. If you get caught in her battalions I cannot help you nor protect you and keep you safe. Do not accept her mark of allegiance then become calloused and hardened against My Voice or your protection will be taken away from you because you have chosen to be on the side of My enemy. If you will pledge allegiance to Me, do it within yourself, then separate your allegiance from the kingdoms of men. My wrath comes forth burning hot with indignation against false shepherds and the system that governs them, blinding My people by their doctrines and traditions.

Woe to you who, just like Judas, thought he could have both and come out a winner. In doing this, he found he could have neither. In crucifying Me, he lost his soul's peace. Then, staring into eternity forlorn and lost, he took his own life.

All those who wish to be a member of both camps will suffer the same loss of peace. I will rid Myself of all spies and double agents in My camp. You cannot evade Me; I govern who enters. For a price you would betray your own soul. Therefore, over to the enemy's camp you go, all you Judases who are double-eyed and double-minded. I will have PURE LOVE in My Sons. They will be kings and priests to Me alone, said Jehovah of old. So do not think you can take Me for a verbal ride while serving yourself behind My back. Submit yourself to My cleansing, otherwise I will submit you to My judgment flame.

Come to Me, all of you. It is critical that you decide now. There is no longer time to wait. It is time to choose. The world will profit you nothing. Even if you owned the whole world you could not buy your soul. Is there nothing worthy to see in Me? Would you rather hang onto your idols? Would you prefer to dream of your success in your lies, myths, and fables? *You do not know the difference between lies and Truth, so why do you think you can decide for yourself what you need?*

Come to Me in your hearts. Give yourself to My cleansing floods of Truth and let My washing regenerate you. To those who bow against Me and think they can hide under falsehood and lies to cover themselves, My overflowing scourge will carry them away and leave nothing behind of their false and sandy foundations. See Me and see Truth...or hear man and wallow with swine. You make the decision. Amen.

My Sword, My Famine, My Pestilence

Woe to the world, its systems, its governments, and all the spirits clinging to them and living under their arm, worshiping the idols of worldly goods.

O world, who will mourn on the day of My visitation to repay you for that which has been done through your establishment and your cherished institutions. Woe to your continents! They will be rent and torn asunder by My Sword. Your present maps will be undone along with all who do not stand with Me, your Redeemer, in these end days of the earth kingdom.

My famine will come upon your fields in repayment for the famine within Christendom and your failure to feed My people My Truth. My words cannot be found in you. You hear them, you sing them, but you do not live them because you have not taken your salvation to heart. You trample My Grace underfoot and sneer at My mercy, seeing My testimony as that of a wimp.

Now it is My turn to show you My power. You will see the power of My Sword, My famine, and My pestilence. I will send these in waves upon your lands, your waters, and the whole of the earth will be undone. If need be, only a small Remnant will escape My anger and be carried into My newly created world. Yes, a new map will be created and the old will be null and void, never again to be remembered by man.

In My new age, all will know of My Grace, My Mercy, and My Love. They will thank Me for having chosen them to escape from the fires of My cleansing. All will know of God and will worship in true humility, having seen the workings of His hand. They will agree as one that He who created this world owns it, and they will give thanks and praise only to Him. All will be truly glad and will remain faithful to His Name after the season of My Sword, My Famine, and My Pestilence.

When this new day comes I will set up governments that are worthy of their calling, and they will follow where I lead. These new organizations will honor My Father's Throne and will not attempt to usurp the power that comes from above. No one will covet a higher seat so that he will look important to men. All will be faithful to the Redeemer and will bless their Creator. I, Jesus, say to you this day that true peace will reign forevermore on the earth after My Sword, My Famine, and My Pestilence.

See, Hear, Say, Do

I, your Redeemer, say to My faithful, who have not yet reached completely perfect purity, seek My Spirit for nourishment and ask continually for My Truth. This will continue your growth toward transformation to Sons and Daughters of God. I say to you, *"See, Hear, Say and Do."*

See Me and acknowledge Me in everything, that I may reward you with abundant fields of wisdom, My pure wisdom which is everlasting. My Truths will reveal all the details of the small and the large, for in maturity you need to understand the importance of each as we continue our journey toward completion. I can only reveal My teachings to those who look and diligently strive to understand.

Do not be slothful or you will not give Me the opportunity to explain and to show the *depths* of Truth. You will remain shallow and subject to every wind of doctrine while remaining confused about their meaning and application within My Kingdom. *See Me*, so I can reward you with My Holy Vision. Only by remaining fixed upon Me could Peter walk on water. This is how it will be with My Sons and Daughters. Come to Me, and I will give you peace to remain focused upon Me and then you can truly be blessed to see.

Hear Me and listen for the Voice of My Spirit always, and I will reward you with pure direction in every circumstance. It will allow you to overcome every hindrance; joy will fill your soul, and confidence will fill your days. Love will expand to extinguish all your fears and doubts, leaving you to travel peacefully along your journey and bring your Light to the Throne of our Father.

Again I say, *Hear Me*, and peace will flow around you in abundant streams, allowing you to find pure truth in all your dealings. My Spirit will bring you to pure levels of communication and keep you upon the path towards maturity. Grace will surround you wherever you are and mercy will forever extend your days. You will never again want to venture into the old, once you truly come to hear Me.

Say Me by speaking only what My Spirit utters in your heart, and I shall bless you with forests of understanding. Holy understanding comes to all who wait and listen for Me to speak to you and through you. Only I know the pure and acceptable answer to all questions, places, and situations; and I long to reward all those who wait for My Spirit to give them My words, so that you can know and in truth *say Me*.

Do Me by obeying every command of My vision, every warning that comes through hearing Me, and following every direction that My Spirit gives you along the journey. If you do this, then you will truly become My Sons and Daughters, stepping into My glory which has existed for all the ages. I desire to give you every good thing, to lead you, to shape you, and bless you with My Power, which overcomes all hindrances and completes you so that My Father's Radiance might be extended upon the earth. Selah! ◆

April 27, 1996

Come to the Light

Children, listen to and learn from My Voice of Teaching. I come to open your eyes to the greatness of My Light of Truth. You have sought Me for understanding, so I come to give you wisdom.

The amount of *selflessness* in you will determine how much I can fill you. *The more you empty yourself of everything from the world, the more I can fill your heart and mind with My words.* You say you do not have much? If this is the case, then you are not giving very much of yourself to Me to fill. Identify with Me and My Kingdom.

This world will not help you. Do not hang onto it, believing it will save you, spare you, or even accept you. If you are Mine, then the world has already rejected you and will continue to do so. Those with the world's mentality will debase, scorn, and ridicule you. It will be no less than My suffering, but neither will it be any greater.

I suffered to death for you, therefore do not be ashamed of Me, Children, but keep yourself relaxed and at peace in the midst of your persecution for My sake.

As it is written, the earth and those who love it will go through great tribulation. Will you who know better and have been warned go along with them because you are afraid of being ridiculed for doing something different?

How many of you have hid the Light of My Spirit under bushels and lost your joy because you fear the sting of condemnation from the ignorant? Was the price for uncovering your Light more than you wanted to pay in terms of your reputation? Are you willing to stand up under this pressure and share My Name, testifying to all, and not just by words but by lifestyle changes? Indeed, which of you offers Me more than lip service? Who does more than talk of obedience, and goes so far as to put their life on My Altar?

Listen to me, Children, My corrections are sorely needed. Examine yourselves in the Light of My Holiness. You were industrious enough to store up savings in the bank to see you through paying your bills, but what about storing up treasures in My Bank? What about offering your heart, soul, and life to Me? Why not give *whole days* to Me, not just an hour here or there? Are you truly Mine or do you just give yourself to My caressing for a short time then snatch yourself back to go chasing after your lusts?

Listen to *yourself*, Children, and evaluate yourselves carefully. Yes, exposure to the Light of My Truth will burn you, but it will only burn away the teachings of the world that should be put to death in order for you to live in wholeness and purity, putting all things to right use before Me. Not all your thoughts, words, or actions will be perfect because you have been raised among the judgments of man. However, hold your heart's motive and intent in a place of love.

If you have a desire to betray your brother, to step on or take advantage of him, you do both yourself and him wrong, and your heart will not be right before Me. If you have hatred and dissonance among you, if there is back biting and fighting, know that My Spirit of Peace cannot live there. When you entertain such thoughts and attitudes, My Spirit is tossed out on the garbage heap as trash while your self-man gloats in his victory and is strengthened.

Woe to you who hold onto and enforce all your "rights," even going so far as to impose them on others. My mercy cannot touch you. On the day of calamity, you will find no mercy from Me. To all you who fight your own battles and get your own revenge I say, "If you gloat in the victory you have won by the strength of your own arm, your hands are stained with the blood of your brother, murdered and tormented by your thoughts, words and actions." Because you would not forgive and demanded punishment, so it will be for you on the day of *your* judgment. So go ahead, gloat over your supposed revenge, but be aware that when it is your brother's turn to get revenge against you, it will not be your brother – it will be the Lord God who will stand in for him and who will exact the revenge in the same measure as you did.

Who in heaven or earth will hear Me and do what I say? My words are everlasting. They are life and health to all them that do as I tell them. I simply tell you what I expect of you, and it is up to you to follow Me wherever you are, whether alone and friendless or in the company of several brethren. You cannot blame each other for your lack on the day when your actions are assessed by My judgment. You will suffer for your unconfessed sins as well as for what you have done in ignorance.[84]

Pray that on the day when it is time to judge how ready you are, you will be found worthy to receive My crown of everlasting life. For now, examine yourself thoroughly and stop deceiving yourself about your inner spiritual condition. And do not overdo what I require from you in obedience.

Your works will mean nothing if you do them because you are compelled to do them out of duty or because you want the admiration of others. What you do must proceed out of your love for Me and your desire to help integrate My Holy Spirit instruction. Otherwise you are amiss with your intention and your works are not eternal, in which case they will be a loss to you. However, you who endeavor to help with good intentions, give yourself wholly to My

---

[84] There are many places in the text where the Lord urges us to "awaken," to "pay attention," or to "be aware." Christ-consciousness is a state of exquisite and unlimited consciousness that is sensitive to every nuance of thought, word, and action, and knows the total effect of these on everyone and everything. To say, "I didn't know he would feel like that…" or "I didn't think that would be the result…" is simply admitting that you have not done the work of cleaning up your thought processes and expanding your consciousness and love. Thus you are not ready for existence in those realms where creation happens immediately in response to what you think and do. This is why Jesus says, "…you would be dangerous…" (see pg. 61)

will for you, presenting your bodies as a *living sacrifice*. When you do this, your work will be sacred and acceptable to Me. If it is done with joy and in My Name, then any suffering that goes with it will bring you the crown of eternal life.

The flesh will profit you nothing, for it is the same as death. What you do not accomplish now in allowing your old self to die you must accomplish on the other side in great sorrow and loss of your inheritance – which is the right to enter My Kingdom.

Therefore, surrender yourself to Me and follow what I am teaching you, for this will save your soul in love. Come to Me alone, wanting to be taught by Me with all diligence, and you will find Me for that is My promise to you, and you can be assured I do not lie to you.

If you cannot find My voice within you, go deeper, seek more intensely. The gods of earth block the flow of your path of receptivity. If necessary, go and sell all you have in order to find Me and earn My favor. Otherwise, you will be choked by the thorns, briars, and the cares of this life. Spend time preparing for the day of My Great Visitation, whereby those who are ready will obtain great joy and honor from Me. Yet those who honor themselves and fancy themselves to be great in My eyes will be disappointed and dishonored and demoted from their high places in front of all.

Heed My warning, all of you My Children, for the Almighty Jehovah has said it and will do it. Amen.

Exhortation to Purity

Awaken fully to My Presence with praise and thanksgiving. Let My grace become evident in your every movement. Do not forget how My mercy was extended to you, and return mercy to all you meet. Let your face shine like the noonday and be a lighthouse in the darkness as My Truth shines forth in the purity of your words and work. Walk with your heads held high in acknowledgement of your forgiveness, and be quick to forgive everyone, for by so doing you continue to be forgiven. Always remember that none of you have attained perfection yet. Thus keep your mind and your efforts on that prize so you will be worthy of its attainment and gifts.

Do not let your understanding be clouded by the cares of the day, by worries about what your future will be, or how future events will unfold. To Me, this is foolish, and it will be a major hindrance to your development in Me.

Your worldly wisdom and efforts to understand will only become a snare to entrap you. Let go of these and trust in Me, keeping yourself humble. A student does not worry about tomorrow's lessons. He is responsible only for fully comprehending the principles being presented today. How can you study ahead of the class when you do not have a copy of My lesson plan – and will *never* have it? It would only bring you pain and cause you to stumble in your conceit. If one knew all the answers, he or she would be drawn to think too highly of their knowledge and would become impatient with the rest of the class, eventually coming to resent the Teacher.

I have stated that we, as a class, would move as quickly as the slowest would allow. In My wisdom I want you to become interdependent and to help each other. Thus, encourage each other and intercede for the others by coming to Me with a request for understanding or assistance that can be shared with them.

You do not know that your strength to overcome comes – and will *only* come – when all are of one accord, seeking understanding as one mind and following the way I direct you. Alone, none of you can stand in the heat of the trials to come, but with My Unity bonding you together as one class, the power to overcome anything will be given to you. Through your actions, love will flow to all. You will learn how to become the least instead of always trying to be the best, as is the way of man. Only by becoming small and humble can you be worthy of the higher positions in My Kingdom. For smallness teaches patience and compassion. It allows you to overcome your old self by seeing, in purity, that your brothers and sisters are cared for *before* serving yourself. That is the way and manner of the Living God – He protects the small and diminishes the proud lofty ones.

You must come to realize, to internalize, that all of you are small before the *I Am* and that He holds everyone equal in His sight and regards no one as above or below another. He watches to see how we treat each other and by so doing, sees how we treat *Him*.[85]

Come unto Me, says your Redeemer, for the time is short and I must retrain you for My purpose. Most lessons will teach you the *total opposite* of man's reactions to situations. Do not be rigid. Allow Me to instruct you and do not hold on to man's instinctive reasoning. Allow yourself to be like a leaf blown in the wind, for the wind of My Holy Spirit will send your group in whatever direction our Father sees necessary until all have been brought to His oneness and made ready to manifest as Sons and Daughters of the Most High.

I declare to all of you that you will certainly face difficulties beyond your strength to endure. You may think you cannot complete the journey and will realize you need the help of your brothers and sisters. So when it becomes evident that one is struggling, reach back, take their hand, and lift them out of the mire, carrying them over their hard spot. By so doing, they will be there in your time of need.

I, your Redeemer, say to the whole class: Do not look around to see which one is ahead or behind. Instead see each as being where I have placed them for now. See only Me and My Spirit, and rejoice over the workings within them. I need honest interdependence among My Sons and Daughters. If you have a problem that is getting the best of you and impeding your growth, talk about it within the group, that all might intercede and hold you up. Do not hide it in embarrassment or shame, for it is My wish that everything will be brought into the open and resolved so it can be overcome and you can move on.

---

[85] See Matthew 25:42-46 for the famous passage that says, *"For I was hungry and you never gave me food; I was thirsty and you never gave me anything to drink; I was a stranger and you never made me welcome, naked and you never clothed me, sick and in prison and you never visited me..."*

Each of you came to this point of convergence by a different path. Each road holds its own unique pitfalls and lessons. By sharing your problems you will gain knowledge of the other's path, and this is important because it is necessary for you as Sons and Daughters to know My workings in each other. Later you will be called upon to deal with My Little Ones *outside* your group, and the knowledge gained here will be invaluable in assessing how to deal with the problems they are struggling with.

Allow Me to teach and instruct each of you, *through each of you and by each of you*, and we will quickly complete our journey to the Light.

April 28, 1996

Purity and Perfection of Heart

The purity and perfection of heart in a person is neither seen nor judged by man. *No* man is able to see it nor is he capable of understanding what I mean by *the perfection of holiness of the heart*, when he insists on looking at the external man and judging the flaws of the human. This is not the right way to judge. You simply do not know how to judge the *nature and character* of an individual as he or she appears to Me in all humility of heart. You cannot even judge your own state of purity or the perfection of your heart. Therefore, how can you know another's? You can know only by what I tell you.

Outward faults or flaws mean little to the *I Am* compared to the heart set. All men make mistakes and have external flaws observable to the one who looks for them. But you do not know, nor *can* you know, more than this at this stage of your development. This is why I tell you, *do not judge your brother or sister, or you will be judged by Me.*

When you do not believe My words about a person because of what YOU think, you have judged. Your disbelief itself will show even you that you have judged. But be aware that when it is My turn to judge, you will be seen as worse in My eyes.

Purity is IN and OF the heart, and the filthiest heart is a self-righteous and judging heart, defiled by hateful thoughts about others. Someone like this can never be considered pure before Me and is cast out of My Presence as vile.

A Prayer for Unity

You are great, O Father. Let us all praise Your Name. You are merciful and righteous in Your judgments towards Your people. Your ways are far above what we can imagine, and You bring joy upon joy without measure to Your Little Ones. Your Grace and Love are like sunshine to our souls, and Your Peace is like a gentle rain upon our parched hearts. Let us remain always prostrate before Your Throne. Incline Your ear to the pleas of Your children and see our petitions as being in right alignment with the will of the Father so that we will be forever welcome in Your Presence.

We thank You for the bountiful blessing of Spirit's guidance. May we wear this guidance like a coat of protection and come to understand Your wisdom as well as Your love for Your people. *You determine what is right and just.* For our part, we will easily ask for what we want, letting go of the outcomes, while we rejoice and praise You for what You bring us. Our fear of Your judgments will lead us and motivate us to follow Your direction, placing no limits on what we are willing to do as we come to see Your Light and plumb the depths of Your understanding.

Do not cast Your people away, but draw us ever closer to You. We will remain humble and loving and will stay open to hear the richness of Your words without grumbling and reservation. Fill us with Spirit and help us hold You in our hearts with love so that You will hold us in Your Heart of Love. Forget our transgressions, forgive our failings, and have mercy on us, Your servants, we pray.

Raise our minds to You in a manner that brings glory and praise to Your Throne, and give us your understanding of what it means to be Your Own. Guide us and direct us along the path to You as You prepare us for Your service, and help us to grasp the lessons You present that we might grow with clarity and certainty, becoming examples of what you want Your Chosen Ones to manifest.

Bring forth our maturity quickly and let Your peace rest quietly on Your Sons and Daughters so there is no division among us. Let Your Light shine brilliantly from each in a oneness that floods the darkness with Your Truth and Love. Amen and Amen.

Unrighteous Judgment

If you look only at the outward actions of a person and judge him accordingly, you are judging unjustly. You think you can judge by someone's deeds, but how can you judge when you cannot read the heart? If a man does not follow your rules and you think badly of him for what he does, you have defiled yourself. In this situation, who is the worst sinner? The man who is not living up to your standards, or you who have defiled yourself by judging your fellow man? What makes one sin different or better than another? What makes you think you have judged rightly when you have been guilty of unloving thoughts and attitudes?

Do not deceive yourself and lie against the Truth. The one who judges his fellow man is worse than the man he judges. The thing that drives you to judge your brother in the first place is nothing other than high-minded conceit. You who cannot see for the log in your own eye should not busy yourself trying to remove the splinter from your brother's eye.

You are a fool. Unless you stop, examine the situation, re-think your position, and cleanse yourself of that self-righteous attitude, replacing it with a humble and loving attitude, you will never enter My Kingdom. You have been warned, and from this point forward, your judgments will turn on you and fall upon your own head.

If I make a man wealthy and he seems more precious than gold, watch your own heart. Do not let it fill with jealousy and anger or My anger will be kindled against you. Stop thinking anxious, unloving thoughts about your brother because all these judgments will be transferred to you. Only the Mighty One judges with equity, fairness, and true righteousness. My judgment falls hard upon all those who judge their brother with a hateful heart and impatient mind.

Do not set yourself up as a judge over your brother man, and beware of putting your brother down so that you can make yourself look better than him. By so doing you make yourself worthy of nothing except My wrath. Pride always leads to a fall, and a haughty attitude will pull you into iniquity and perverseness. Let all who seek to judge their brother understand that you will not escape My judgment. Your inheritance will be removed and your pride ground to a powder for daring to so insult My Authority. Listen, because the wrath of God falls upon the children of disobedience.

Vanity

Do you judge others because of vanity and competition? Is your eye critical and your mind insulting toward those that do not dress like you? Think about it …what *IS* clothing? Is it not simply to cover your nakedness? Can you see that when you judge others by the way they dress you are holding wickedness within your own heart? Are you judging others because their outward appearance does not exhibit the fine taste or pleasing mannerisms that you lust for yourself?

And who has the right to judge someone's weight? Who sets the standard for all men about this? Does their weight show you the heart of a person? Can you use *this* measure to judge accurately? *No!* Beware, you that like to judge, for your heart is not in the right place or in alignment with Me. I will expose your wickedness and lusting, so listen and fall on your faces before Me, lest My wrath come upon you for your perverseness.

Christendom, like the Pharisees of old, teaches that neatness and fineness of dress, demeanor, and taste are a rule and a standard. I sent the Pharisees the rugged John, the evangelist who baptized, to offend their manner of fine clothing, who did not eat sumptuously, who did not dwell not in fine palaces, but was rough and rugged and barely dressed. I had groomed him, but not in the ways they expected. Because he did not eat their fine foods nor drink their wine, they did not approve of him.

I say to you, as I said to John, "What do you go out to see? A person arrayed in fine, soft clothing? They live in king's palaces. No, I send you a burning, shining Light, like I am, and you are offended at them." Do not take part in unrighteous judgments with others or within yourselves, and do not judge My servants or you will be judged as guilty of blasphemy.

For you who think you are so wise, know that I come again and again in ways unacceptable to your pride. Again, I challenge your authority, and again you are offended. Where you should have acted in humility and meekness, you showed yourselves to be arrogant and proud. First you murder My witnesses in your hearts, then outwardly as well, showing yourselves to be false.

The mark of The Beast is in your own heart, and it will soon find itself outwardly expressed. Do not lie to yourselves, Shepherds, for I have come to take back whatever you have stolen and to pay you back for all those you have deceived and lied to. You will feel great heat from My wrath. Hear My words and lament, for the beauty and profitability of Christendom and its coffers will be taken away by My destroying Sons, who will come forth full of My Spirit and create your destruction. You are marked for destruction by your attitude. I hold you responsible for the loss of so many of My lambs by your lies and perverseness.

My glaring, white-hot Light of exposure is focused on you, Christendom. Wherever you dwell in the hearts of men, O spirit of whoredom, you will be exposed. And in your exposure you will lose your power, for the Lord of the Most High has declared it. Amen.

Man vs. *I Am*

God says to you: Today I have determined how I will rule in regard to the matter of *man vs. I Am*. I have found all of you to be in a state of disbelief. There are none among you who really understand or are knowledgeable about Truth. Therefore, I will extend My mercy to you and will remain extended until My rivers of pure Living Water have had a season to cleanse man of man's ideas. Not until then will I consider the matter of original transgression.

My Son and My Holy Spirit will offer instruction in ways pleasing to Me so that you may add your Light to the fullness of My Radiance. At the end I will determine individually how you have received this extended grace. I will plow your fields, turning under their thorns and briars and will return to all who will receive from My hand a planting of goodness and Truth.

If you will submit to My Guidance and express My Love to every creature I have created, you will see and know My mercy. I will deal with those who will not receive Me later in the day when I declare, "Let he who is righteous continue to be so, and let he who is unrighteous remain so evermore. Then My fires will consume all who reject My infinite mercy." Those vessels fit for destruction will be cast away by their own choice and their own desires.

Amen, I say, come to Me while the door is still open. Look at what man is doing to his brothers and sisters and change your ways. Come to Me and be washed of the stains of your humanity. Come and be restored to the good Vine while I allow you time. You do not know when My Door will close. In the day of Noah, I recognized only eight as belonging to Me. Using this tiny remnant I began again, starting fresh and new. From them I issued a pure stream of My own making. Once again I will do the same thing on your earth. I will be their God – their only God – and they will be My people, pure and redeemed by Me, joining Me and My Throne evermore.

Let all of you remain prostrate and silent before the Throne of the Almighty until all this has been fulfilled and you have reached your completed status as a Son of God.

Mighty Harlot, Christendom

How is it that you, O Christendom, expect to be approved in My sight? This expectation is really an example of you approving of yourself then attributing it to Me. What is growing within your breast? O mighty harlot, you will be exposed, and this exposure will be your demise, for The Beast that now carries you will turn on you and destroy you once you have been laid bare in front of everyone's eyes.

Listen to Me, O People: *flee her gates*. Do not come near her doors, for the *I Am* has proclaimed her iniquity to you. Flee from her influence, her bewitching fear-producing curses, and do not cling to her any longer. There is still time for your path to be decided, although the day is almost here when you will no longer have time to choose. Get up and move into My camp, or you will be judged as one of her followers.

Watch and be aware! My threat is serious. I do not blow this trumpet for vanity's sake. I am only sounding an alarm throughout Christendom to let you know that you have been cut off from My grace and mercy. The result will be a judgment waiting for you when the time comes for judgment to fall. Hear Me, People. Flee from her influence and come to My dimensions of Life. Your own private prayer closet is enough for you. There is safety only under My wing.

So come, and do not wait to yield to Me. There is much to be taught and learned, and you will be able to raise your consciousness to My level according to your diligence. Understand that I pay no attention to the faces of men or their proud and vain clothing. I am not moved by their bribes or their attempts to bargain with Me. I demand Truth, which is found only in your inner self. I demand a life ruled by true justice and a heart of love and equity.

Blessed are the peacemakers. Cursed are all the peace takers. Your world is a world of darkness, iniquity, and perversion – and you are satisfied with this. Be aware that all of you are constantly transgressing the Love, Truth, Wisdom, and Peace that lives within you. You cannot believe that these things are within you and instead express fear, hate, anger and lies. I might yet have some mercy upon you, but if you shake your fist at Me or get angry and despise My words, beware. I do not forget anything, and you who are haughty will end up having to submit to My cleansing fire of Truth either on this side or on the other.

To you who understand and believe, there will come great relief. The mercy of the Father works for the souls of all men, for He created them all so they would learn to worship Life and live in eternity, giving thanks forever. Amen.

Tearing Down Strongholds

My little flock, arise and come into My presence with praise and thanksgiving. Yes, let My cleansing streams of Love flow over you and through you that My joy will fill you as well.

Today I will again return to the realm of stewardship and your desire to learn My Truth. Can you see that each week I am building upon the week before? Let us review: First I gave you *resurrection, rebirth, and renewal.* Now I present the tearing down of strongholds – both within you and in the outer world – that are hindering the growth of My Kingdom in you and in your world.

Earlier I asked each of you to enter the private closet of your study and to allow Me to show you *individually* how you regard the words I have given you in the past. Did you do as I commanded? Be honest with yourselves for I already know the answer. Did you re-read those newsletters so you could receive the blessing I promised? How do you receive the words given to you today? Do you receive My instruction with gladness? Do you hunger and thirst to find Me within yourself?

If you do not allow Me to fully inhabit your body/mind and individually give you My blessings, there will be no growth, no maturity, and Sonship[86] must be delayed, to your detriment and Mine. If you need refilling and renewal you must ask for it. Open the door, otherwise I cannot come in and give you the thirst and the hunger necessary to bring you to completion. Do not do as some do and toss aside My fresh and current words, thinking you will read it later. My words are for that moment when given, and if you toss them aside for later, not only will they not make as much sense to you, you will never get the blessing of My full meaning and understanding. See it as "learning delayed is learning lost." When your mind is far from Me and caught up in your own cares, you can neither learn from Me, nor care for Me or the things I want to teach you.

It cannot be this way if you want to reach full maturity in Me, and none who are slothful in My employment will be stewards of Mine. Thus, check yourselves and come to Me so I can make you fruitful before Me and before My Father's Throne.

Come unto Me and allow My Spirit to come to you so that we may be as one. Yes, one mind, one heart, one soul, and one body, pure and cleansed of all negative thoughts, words, and actions, giving all credit to the Father and thanking His Holy Name.

---

[86] *Sonship* refers to a level of existence that we often think of as "the realm of the gods." It is a very high level of consciousness in which the beings who reach it aren't just made of light or filled with light, they begin to *generate* Light from within.

Forgiveness, Mercy & Love

God is radiant glory and Intelligent Light; let us all praise His Holy Name. Let no one else be praised, glorified, or magnified other than the *I Am*. His Risen Son asks His Children to constantly praise and give thanks to our Father from whom all blessings flow. Let there be the same Love and Abundance on earth as there is in Heaven.

Today I give to you My Promise that love will gush forth from you like a wellspring for your souls. Yes, for a little while the door of mercy will be open. Consider the Father's wisdom. Let it fully consume you and fill your entire body and mind:

> *Forgiveness is better than vengeance,*
> *Mercy is better than anger, and*
> *Love is better than judgment.*

All of the former – Forgiveness, Mercy, and Love – are everlasting and will bring you to your Father's goodness and glory. All of the latter – vengeance, anger and judgment – lead to destructtion and damnation. Look within yourselves to see where your thoughts reside. A pure body/mind always does good and a polluted one always does harm even when it is trying to do good, because the heart is not right.

Mixtures of good and harm drive My Little Ones away from My hand. All mixtures must be cleansed completely. They will not last eternally and will never enter into heavenly realms. Growth is determined by the implementation of heavenly principles *while you are still walking upon the earth*. It is in this manner that a little bit of Heaven is brought down to men.

Do those things which are everlasting and you will be blessed all of your days. Do those things which destroy or hinder My work and I promise you, damnation will be your reward. Your days will be cursed with confusion and uncertainty, both in the earth and forevermore. Mixtures cause you to be double-minded, looking to Me part of the time, looking to men part of the time, and this will leave you in a position of being accepted by neither and tormented by both.

Come to Me with your mind devoted exclusively to receiving the fullness of My intended salvation for you. When you do, joy will replace your despair, peace will quiet your confusion, hope will wash away your uncertainty, My love will fill you eternally, and My grace will not have been given to you in vain. Amen and Amen.

Chosen Sons & Daughters

I call many to Me but few choose to listen or follow Me into their own potential fullness. Those who choose to come to Me are not those whom man regards highly nor are they the ones that mankind rewards as successful on the earth. Often, those I call "My Chosen" are people you have not even attempted to receive or understand. The path that My chosen follow can seem peculiar, even strange, to all man has been taught and holds dear.

Man never attempts to see beyond the outer facade. He knows nothing of the inner life and cannot understand My unseen workings, nor can he believe beyond the measure of his parent's understanding… at least not until now.

However, I will show those who choose Me the inner powers that manifest through My Sons and Daughters. Yes, all will know who is Mine, yet none of My Chosen will say it is them. Nevertheless, My everlasting principles will flow from them and guide them. Yes, all the world will be astonished, then ashamed, and will want to know how to become peculiar and strange for their own sakes! They will flee from their former beliefs and customs, and I will receive them into Myself. In doing this, My reign will be established in the end days and made available to all who are willing to receive.

The old, stale, dry, and unfulfilled ways will not continue to drive their desires nor prevent their progress as they are drawn to Me.

They will be attracted by the power manifested by My Sons and Daughters as I am poured out through them and by them. All who take part in Me will share in the growing radiance of the Light within.

Rejoice and be thankful today. Let your joy be filled to overflowing. Through joy you can rise above all that anchors you here below. Come higher…yes, become lightened and enlightened, as your cares and problems are released to ME.

Praise me with tongues, and let your spirit plead your case when words fail you. *This is the way to constant communion which I desire for you* and which My Spirit provides to you. Yes, Spirit is an avenue to rise above all that troubles or hinders you and robs you of your joy.

Heaven's Ambassadors

My little ones, have you remembered that My righteousness is your righteousness – and this makes you citizens of the Kingdom of Heaven and only pilgrims and strangers here on the earth? So why do you allow yourselves to be robbed of your rightful inheritance by clinging to dual citizenship? Today I ask you to choose only one. Will you be of the Kingdom of the air, or will you remain captured in the kingdom of the dust? How can you be Heaven's ambassadors if you do not allow yourselves to be subject to its laws, practices, and customs? How can you convey these to the world if you do not know what they are and cannot exhibit them? Come to Me, for only I can teach you how to represent Heaven's government correctly. *This can only be achieved by constant communion with Me, unhindered by your additions or subtractions.* An ambassador only says what his King bids him to say, only does what his King bids him to do, and only goes where his King sends him.

Seek the heavenly Kingdom and its glorious radiant Light. Do not be drawn under the hand of earthly kings, rulers, and popes, for they are all carnal, temporal, and will pass away.

Surrender All

Do not withhold yourself from Me, for My light of self-examination is *for your good*. I reveal to you what is necessary for you to grow. Do not withhold yourself because you are afraid that what you see will hurt. Instead, know that withholding yourself is what will hurt you. I can only occupy and cleanse those parts you *willingly surrender* to Me. My Spirit longs to cleanse you completely, then fill you quickly before your old self attempts to re-take the throne of your heart.

There is nothing hidden from Me, for I know all your shortcomings. Yes, all of you have them. They are inherent to your human nature. Do not be ashamed, for I have not come to criticize or belittle, but rather to uplift the downtrodden, to give peace of mind to the depressed, and to inform all regarding Myself in hopes that everyone can become functional with My gifts from Spirit.

So come to Me and I will give you great rewards – not punishment – when you surrender all to Me. Yes, I love all of you with an everlasting love and want you to come to maturity quickly.

The Kingdom of Love

The advancement of the Kingdom of Love occurs when the kingdom of men's lust, the kingdom of darkness and dust, has been put in the grave and buried. There can be no mixing of the two, their statutes or their customs. Neither can your expensive buildings serve in My New Kingdom. All must be brought to nothing so that the *I Am* may reign in purity.

Thus, let all that was born of the kingdom of darkness be laid waste in you. Let all your old and beloved theology and theocracy be cast aside so that My New might replace it. You will see new life as soon as you are ready. I have bountiful blessings and liberty for you as soon as you yield to My Authority. But wherever you hold onto the old, you cannot receive My New. Submit your toys and substitutes for Truth so I may give you the REAL AND TRUE SUBSTANCE, INCLUDING MYSELF.

As it is written in this book, I come to do My Father's good pleasure and to root out all things that offend Him so that I may raise up Sons and Daughters like Me. Therefore, hear My Voice all you candidates and surrender your hearts to Me, forsaking the domains and dominions of Christendom for My Sake, that you may be found worthy in My sight to receive My revelation.

For I love you and I take no pleasure in the death of the wicked. I see no great benefit in mass slaughter nor does destruction please Me. Yet, in your sins you have pressed Me beyond measure, and the earth groans under the strain. Therefore, I must and will bring vindication of My Eternal Throne. The earth must and will adjust itself, according to what you have done to it, and this you must also suffer.

From here forward, do not cling to idols (even of the heart) and think that they can rise and save you, for I say to you, they cannot. They are not gods. Thus do not wait until your situation is dire to find out you've been deceived and that you trusted in lies, for then you will find you do not have the grace and mercy to endure. Make your choice and come to Me, asking to be used for My Service.

My Great Purpose

Let your eye be focused upon Me alone, and clear your sight of everything except My Great Purpose, which I will not back down from for any man or men. I come to liberate My captives during this the day of Vengeance, says the Eternal One. Long ago I decided that My Purpose would not be deterred by any ways and means of men, but would go forward in order to redeem My Little Ones who remain captives of the darkness and the veil of blindness spread over all nations. Thus I come to produce the promised inheritance to My people.

When I come to you and My Light of Truth dawns in you and through you, share it with others. Receive this healing Light deeply into your being. Allow My cleansing Flame to cut away the foreskin of your heart, for that is the true and real circumcision.

I am ready to begin birthing My Sons into the gladness of My Creation where they will be delivered from the great curse of Adam's sin upon it. As you have seen birth pangs in your own opening to Spirit, know that your earth must ALSO suffer them to bring forth My newly re-created place and to establish My Reign in the end days.

Submit your knowledge to Me, yes, all that you have, and be willing to let Me sift and sort through it, taking some out or leaving some in according to My own wisdom. I will tear down old foundations within you. Yet trust and have confidence that I will return all to you straightened and purified. A new picture will appear to you, where you now have a jumbled one.

Do not seek to predict anything about My Coming for *it will not be done in the same manner to all*. Therefore do not seek to exhibit wisdom when, in truth, you do not have any. Instead be humble and flexible, constantly asking Me what is best and what I would say or do.

Praise and thank Me again and again, for this will keep you focused on Me. Hold no one, no servant of Mine, as more important than other people and let your words and action come as directed by ME ONLY, so that My Father may be glorified and Life strengthened within you. The pride of man will completely fall, and humility will reign among My Soldiers.

Bring out the anointing oil and anoint My Servant who has just come among you this day, Willie, for you are his brother in truth, and Truth will come from you to him. Seek Me forever, Soldiers of My Cause, and look for the greatness of My Kingdom. Amen.

Wellspring of Life

"The valve of Love's spigot is opening to you. Ask constantly to receive a greater flow," says the Eternal Wellspring from on High. For I am a wellspring of Life and you are all dry, thirsty sponges in need of refreshing with the Water of Life. Know that I need you and want to show you the great Light inside you that you may see the potential given to you and begin to use the talents I gave you. Do not hide them, for this will be to your own shame and disgrace.

I come with recompense for all, both good and bad, in equity and in righteousness. Where you have followed Me, you will be blessed. Where you have looked to men for answers and direction, you have lost ground. Listen to My admonition: HOLD FAST TO WHATEVER PROGRESS YOU HAVE MADE SO THAT NO MAN STEALS YOUR CROWN AND REWARD.

Hand of Mercy or Justice?

Shall I judge with a hand of mercy? Or shall I judge with a hand of justice? Surely they are much the same, yet viewed differently by mortals, depending on the Light (understanding) they have.

The church that is called Christendom senses My hand coming upon it. It will be seen as mercy to those who are trapped there and as justice by those who have been hurt by them. As My hand goes forth, Christendom will show that she does not know Me and will call Me *Evil, Satan,* and *Devil.*

Once again, she will not see who I am and will seek to silence all those who speak for Me. She will throw up her bars and gates to imprison the sheep still within her. And she will lay down stringent rules and guidelines of association in her efforts to spare herself a great loss of followers and profit.

Nevertheless, to My hungry, thirsting lambs, My extended hand will look like mercy as I speak about the exposure of she who is false and in need of destruction. Many will rush with great joy to follow ME.

REMEMBER AND UNDERSTAND that I have *many* beloved sheep inside Christendom, who are imprisoned by tradition and do not know it. I constantly search it with candles and relight the tiny sparks who are indeed Mine. I do not sacrifice a single one of My beloved sheep, but allow each to make their decision. In this way I am *just,* I am *fair*, and I am *loving* to all who want Me.

My Peace

May the peace of My Father be upon you, My Beloved Children, peace the world cannot know, peace and calm and relief from all stress. I give each of you hope in Me and also deliverance. Deliverance from what? From all your fears. Your fears are like chains. Your worries are like strongholds of an enemy. Behold, I am Eternal. I am not a being who was created to be ruled by fear. Thus, I come with My Key of Love to unlock your chains of fear that lead to death.

Hold your hearts up to Me and let Me shine My Light into you. Let Me warm your ground which I have planted with seeds that are growing and which I have blessed so they will be fruitful. Let your harvest be a blessing for Me.

In the same way that a seed gives up its old life, your willingness to ignore and let go of your old self will allow the potentials of Life to spring forth many times over. For by death to self comes Life multiplied.

From Whence Springs Life?

Where does Life come from? And especially, where does Eternal Life spring from? From the world? From people? From the knowledge of men? NO. Life, *PURE LIFE*, is found in only One place – your Redeemer, who pours his or her Life through you and from you to all via your anointed prophetic pens. From now on, all will hear My Guidance. All will be able to make a choice to follow or to ignore and disobey.

Do you think I am right in this manner? Who are you, O men and women, to decide this? I use whom I can. I raise up those who are willing to empty out all they have been for My sake. As for those who are not ready yet, I must labor on until they enter My purifying fire. I mold those whom I can.

Each of you is a vessel, thus be willing and pliable in your usefulness to Me each day that we come together. Because of this I love you and labor with great earnestness. Amen.

Do not let death overwhelm or overshadow you, for My work is not finished, even though thoughts of returning to your busy life troubles My Spirit in your midst. I want you all to flow together and have no other will than Mine and to be in My Presence, which is peace, forevermore.

Learn to stand in the Presence of My white-hot fire of cleansing which will cleanse you of everything and purify your mind of all except Love, Joy, and Truth.

Life Flows Forth

Life flows through you, My open conduits, like water through rivers and streams, satisfying you, O My thirsty Ones. Therefore, receive My Water of Life and drink deeply of Me, for this will save your "house," making it a *resurrected* one. With patience you will possess your souls. Amen.

Power Upon Power

My Servants, your willingness to honor Me by giving Me your time so I can teach you is eternal work which cannot be shaken. It will remain forever in your heart and the hearts of others who receive and benefit from its outflow and can never be done away with.

Power upon power is multiplied through the words you receive in dictation. I will come to bless and receive many people through your willing service. In this, your work is everlasting and eternally beneficial to all. Think on these things!

Street Kids

The Lord says that He will pick children off the street corner and they will [be willing to] serve the Lord with all their hearts. People will look at these children and say, "Not so!" But I say to you that it *will* be so. I pick those who will serve Me, and this includes children who have been abused and given over to the devil. I know the hearts of men and mankind. Know this…that My manifested Sons will bless them about the streets. Amen.

Let My River of Love Flow

To My children whom I dearly Love I say: Do not give any time, attention, or power to your past experiences. Do not focus on future events and worries. Be full of joy in the *PRESENT* and let My River of Love flow through you.

O My Children, Listen only to Me, so we can conquer every one of the enemies, the small and the big. All will be washed away from the vessels I clean. I am the Cleansing Fire who will burn out all corruptions and free you from captivities by the enemies forever.

Beloved, be Mine forever, coming to Me with all your holdings. Offer up everything every day, every toy you play with, so we do not have anything holding and slowing your growth.

My New Millennial

Gentlemen, are you ready to enter My New Millennial? Are you ready for the purging that will become evident? The Messiah, the Eternal One, says it is nearly upon you.

Come into your closets. Find rest and peace in Me, and allow the wisdom of My Holy Spirit to come to you. Without the revelation that comes to you from the Christ within, you are lost and will never know the truth of My Gospel. This revelation will help you understand it. Therefore, listen and do not fight against it in your ignorance. Submit yourself to Me, handing over whatever you think your cause might be and however many and varied your beliefs are. I will overturn, overturn, overturn everything, leaving man's great inventions upside down and testing the works of men until they have been proven, even if I must do so by fire.

The flame and the sword are upon you, O people. Hear My Trumpet of war and become Soldiers for My cause, laying your own wills aside. The enemy comes in great fury against My Light, to do away with many. The dragon rises up to take many good lives away.

Hear My Trumpet and be wise. Do not run to the world. Come to Me in prayer and seek to understand. The day of My Vengeance is coming, and there will be a purge of all that is false.

If you do not believe *Me*, then believe for the sake of the words I tell you so that you do not reject the revelation I bring you. Listen and hear and your soul will live, says the Lord of Glory. There are few candidates among men who are willing to join My Mighty Army. Nevertheless it will be sufficient to bring forth and fight My Cause.◆

April 29, 1996

Man's Love vs. God's Love

Blessed be the God and Father of our Lord Jesus Christ. When we seek Him and allow the Father to use us, we grow *in Him and the things of His Holy Spirit*. He will raise our hearts, our eyes and our minds up to Him, especially if we are small and humble, and even if we think we are foolish.

Blessed be the one who walks in love towards his brothers and his sisters, for he will be a savior to them and a helping hand that offers no shame or guilt. He will offer unconditional Love, which is the Love of the Eternal. The world does not know unconditional love and can neither duplicate nor produce it in ways that will benefit all. Love – True Love – is found only in those who focus on the Pattern of Christ, who *is* Love and the Author of all that is and ever will be.

Bless and hold the love that flows among your group and know the Source of that Love. It comes from God, not from man. True Love loves, even when one falls. It is offered in ways that do not shame others, seeks to lift up the head that has begun to hang down, works to restore the dignity lost by the fall, and encourages the sorrowing one to right all wrongs. When this kind of help is offered, the growth and return of the fallen one is fast!

In contrast, man's restrictive nature is demanding, proud, haughty, and severe toward those who make mistakes or fall from grace. O what beatings, scourging by the tongue, and lashings with every kind of judgment and self-righteous thoughts he offers! This is not love. It is hate, masked as love and helpfulness, which can restore no one and only leaves them in bitterness and anger. My flocks have received this kind of treatment at the hands of evil shepherds who are more correctly referred to as "wolves," biting and tearing at My sheep. They are hirelings who do not care for My flock. They only care for their salary and benefits, while their "services" rob My people in great selfishness.

My House is a house of prayer! Again you have made it a den of robbers and thieves! Depart from Me all you who work only with iniquity, perversity, and lies! Once exposed, you will be destroyed by My Destroying Sons! Learn the difference between My Love and man's love and do not be not fooled any more.

Darkness In Your Midst

The glory and the unity of My people stands as a testimony to My Spirit of Peace among them. When the peace is disrupted by evil thoughts of envy and jealousy, the darkness strikes out at My Light of Love. In patience, love takes and receives this, yet loves in return.

When darkness is threatened it moves into a corner or hides itself in a closet for a while, but it survives to strike again, and this will be the case until darkness ceases to operate in the midst of each of your kingdoms.

The darkness tries to usurp My Power so it can again teach and lead and control. It wants to think its own thoughts of judgment and malice, unmolested by My Truth which it disdains. It rejoices when Truth falls hard and seeks to see it go down.

I counsel you, Children, give no place to darkness. Do not let it gain entrance and strength in your heart and mind. You control the "dimmer switch" of the Light you allow in your own heart-rooms. You will see for yourselves how much you allow the Light to reign in you. The darkness tries to work its ruin of Me within your brothers and sisters and strikes out to challenge and punish My Saints, your brethren. Thus be Light within yourselves and tolerate no darkness. Keep your eyes focused only on Me and My beautiful Light forever, for I will strengthen and season your group. Amen.

April 30, 1996

A Purging Cometh

I have always spoken according to My Holy Spirit within man in successive generations. I have always taught openly. Yet the darkness of the world hurries to cover up the fact that I was behind each situation where Truth and Light was revealed. So in a direct way, there was always a purging, a genocide of innocents, all because of My revelations, which attacked the established religious order.

Once again I come to bring you revelation. And once again the darkness of your world will try to cover over and dissipate My Light. But know that it cannot be done. For this time I will spread My Light of Revelation all over and in every corner. You will come to the Light generated by My Rising and will be judged accordingly. Pray that the light that exists in you does not darken so you will be protected from suffering great loss.

The purging will be unsuccessful, nevertheless it will take place as the serpent of darkness manifests against the Light of My Purpose.

Quiet yourselves, O people, and commune with your hearts in your bed. The Lord comes in judgment upon all who claim to honor His Name vainly in order to lie to the people and steal from them.

Behold and be aware! I come, and My reward is with Me – a reward that leads to life or the curse of death. Choose *life* so that you will live, and do not give your days to the serpent of destruction. Do not pass your time in lascivious judgment. Do not look down noses of arrogance. For behold, the Lord God comes quickly. His Trumpet is blowing the alarm of war against you, O Christendom. Listen to its thunder. The world will be a different place now that the time of My Vengeance has arrived. Hear Me, I do not lie. Come to My peace while you can.

Sure Current Words

The Most High pleads with men to take hold of Him with all their strength and seek His direction and guidance constantly. His current words hold sure guidance. They lead you to be ever mindful of His training and the purpose for which He created you. The actions of counterfeit teachers are seductive, even addictive to your nature. For the love of fellowship, many of His beloved sheep have choked themselves off from Life and become unfruitful.

The Lord says, "You must forsake the entire world, even the good religious parts of it, to win Me." There can be no idols of the heart, not even teachers. My word is clear; do not stray from Me and go chasing after other gods or lovers. For I am your FIRST LOVE. Where you have lost Me, you suffer in darkness. Life becomes dry, and you are left with only husks to eat. Do not *pretend* to return to Me while preferring to keep the teachers you idolize and cherish. You must be willing to believe what your eyes cannot see in your blind obedience, and recognize when evil fruit is growing.

Listen inside for the Voice of My Instruction and learn to receive what I say. *I speak from within you* so that you no longer rely on the unfaithfulness of teachers who do not know Me nor do they walk upon My Highway of Holiness.[87] All that Christendom has taught you must be unlearned and relearned according to Holy Spirit guidance. The veil of darkness covering all nations and people is about to be ripped off to the amazement of all and the consternation of Christendom. When that day comes, she will experience her ruin and the loss of many of her followers. Indeed, she looks fair and righteous on the outside, but she is the *bondwoman*. Flee from her influence, O Sons and Daughters, and hide under My wings.

Carnal wisdom will do you no good and on the last day will be burned with fire until nothing remains. Pray that you will be

---

[87] Isaiah 35:8 describes a highway called "The Sacred Way" traveled only by those who have learned to keep their thoughts, words, and deeds in perfect alignment with the Yahweh.

worthy of some jewels and gems from Me, that your loss not be complete. Good ideas will not help man nor will the strength of numbers and/or votes. What man has created will fall *completely*.

May 1, 1996

One Mighty Shepherd

Do you fear that natural events or accidents will take away the ones you love? The Lord is a Mighty Shepherd. The only helpful fear is fear of Him, for this will lead you away from death into the blessings of eternal Life.

Hear O Israel, The Lord your God is ONE LORD. Listen to Him. On the mount of transfiguration they saw only Jesus transfigure himself, yet afterwards they wanted to build a shrine for each of the three who were there – Jesus, Moses, and Elijah. The Father said: This is My Beloved Son – Hear Him! So *do this* if you want to find life. He is the Author of Life and of Peace and shows us the way to find these.

You haughty ones – listen! There is but *one* God, and it is not you. Come down from your self-made pedestals and become humble before your God. If you do, He will raise your consciousness to the Kingdom of the Most High.

For many people, doubts cause a shadow to fall over the path to Me. Thomas had this problem and that is why I said to him: "Blessed are your eyes for they see and believe. But *more blessed* are they who have not seen and yet believe." Amen.

The Father is looking for followers who will learn to worship only Him, in spirit and in truth. Go to Him believing, and you will receive what you ask for.

Keep your mind on him and focus on love and forgiveness. He who saves up wrath, anger, and doubt will receive nothing from the Most High except rebuke.

Hear O Israel! Respect the Lord God, who made heaven and earth, and do not think He is a fool like many men. His ways and thoughts are much higher than your ways and thoughts. The proud He criticizes and embarrasses, but He lifts up the head of the humble. You have not known Him or His ways. You ended up following the advice of strangers, walking a path that was not good, and went backward instead of forward.

The teachings of man have been a snare and a trap, leading you into deception. You have followed every man, copying his ways to your destruction and peril. Generations have risen and fallen pursuing an evil course, walking in the way that was not good, and have been devoured by the curse of death. Awaken, and turn to Me once more, for why would you want to die, O My People? Choose *Life* and live. Practice the ways of the Almighty, for indeed He is the Mighty Shepherd and atones for you all.

Listen to Him and no other, lest you be led astray. Men who set themselves up to look like gods have turned your head and enticed you to follow them. You did not know that they led you away from Me, down a path that was not good – the broad, wide, easy way that leads to death.

Correct yourself while there is still time. Your Master pleads with you to return to Him. You do not know the wickedness of Christendom that His eye can discern. Save your life by following the voice of your True Shepherd. Turn to Him and receive life for your prayers. LOVE ONLY GOD. There is no other "right way."

When He says, "Have no gods before Him," He means that nothing and no one should be more important than the *I Am* and the messages of the Christ to you. Trust Him to lead you to His Kingdom by the straight and narrow gate. All those who find it find Life.

There are many who can be heard calling out to the Lord who then do not let Him lead them. Instead, they trust in men as worthy guides. These men speak of themselves and their own shallow, carnal, earthly wisdom. Who does this glorify – God or men? The Father within speaks from heaven, offering wisdom of the ages. *Hear Him and live*, like we did in the beginning.

I have sent Jesus to lead you. He has sent the Comforter, the Spirit of Truth to be your Inner Teacher.[88] Do not trust in man, whose breath is in his nostrils. Flee into your inner closet, the secret place of the Most High, and breathe the breath of Spirit, trusting in the shadow of His wings.

Turn to Him from whom you have revolted, and He will have pity and heal you. Do not cast yourselves away in your ignorance, for this is a blight upon your souls. Though you have many shepherds, you are like untended sheep. Therefore hear the voice of your True Shepherd and turn again to Him who will lead you to green pastures. Beside His still waters you will find peace. Do not turn to teachers who promise a better way, for they know nothing and work only deception, bringing forth the ways of death.

They are flamboyant and you can see it. There is no meekness or lowliness. Why don't you seek the Pattern of meekness and lowliness for your learning? Then you cannot make a mistake. My true ones are not taught in seminaries; they are taught only *at My feet*. They do not learn the ways of the world or stand in the ways of Egypt, Christendom, or Babylon.

Turn to Him from whom you have revolted. Even from heaven I would be able to hear you and heal your land. But you are divided into your divisions, and by division you are made weak. In the time of My Coming, you will all fall down together even though

---

[88] See John 14:16-28 to read of Jesus efforts to make the apostles understand that there was a Being within each of them that could teach them and lead them to "The Father," which is the principle of Life, and which, if they came into full alignment with it, would allow them to do the kinds of miraculous things Jesus demonstrated.

you are joined hand in hand. So turn again to Me, says the Mighty Shepherd, or else there is no hope for you. Christendom will be judged by Me, and that, *shortly.*

BEHOLD, I AM THE *I AM*. I CHANGE NOT. Therefore, *hear* and *know* and *come to Me. If you want to stand in My Presence, then make nothing more important than Me.*

All the gods of earth separate you from Me and you cannot enter into My world. Cast away your idols of money and gold, people and possessions, and come, naked and bare to Me in your hearts. Forgive, unless you want to be unforgiven. Humble yourself before the Lord God and let Him lift you up.

Come into His presence singing, giving thanks to His Name. The Lord is good and merciful to those who seek Him and His Kingdom of Love, Righteousness, and Justice. Those who act on their own ideas of righteousness and rely on earthly works and laws will lose His Presence until they return to Him.

May 3, 1996

The Spirit of Jezebel Described

The Spirit of Jezebel is a powerful spirit that loves wickedness under the guise of goodness and seeks to use it on others. Hidden behind an outer cloak or act of holiness and piety, there is an inner desire for a position of power that overwhelms the person to the point that she seeks to manipulate everything in order to have her way.

Though the gods worshiped by this spirit are of "Belial" or the flesh world, those aligned with it claim great knowledge of Christ and of God. She is totally deceiving. She thinks she is serving God the Almighty but she is only serving herself. She tries to make everyone serve her out of respect for her wisdom, knowledge, and experience. She has a hateful heart, inwardly defaming others. She rules and, with such a spirit, will stop at nothing to have her way and dream fulfilled, using others as pawns that are sacrificed to get what she wants.

Anyone falling under her influence beware! She becomes "god-like" before you and you fall at her feet in obedient worship, thinking she is a great one.

The humility of the Lord's true servants is not found in such a person, whether male or female. The spirit of Jezebel is about serving whichever god is most convenient. All of Christendom is under her influence. Many seek to benefit from her ways.

The Lord says: *"I will throw her into a bed, and they that love her will be thrown into great tribulation, unless they repent."*[89] She has doctrines that embrace many different teachers and theories. Nothing can stop her from reaching her goals but death. She rises upon the broken backs of humanity and its goodwill. She sustains herself on the blood of true prophets and regularly murders true brothers in her heart in efforts to puff herself up. She is Satan's bride and pride and, as the Lord had no mercy on her prophets of Baal, neither will show them mercy in our day and time. The Lord says to flee from her influence and reject her ideas and strong desires. She is the spirit of whoredom working her witchcraft on others, and her power is bound to Satan and his priests of satanic power. The only difference between them is that this one walks in Christendom, therefore is not deemed a "witch."✦

---

[89] In Revelation 2:20-23 John complains that the self-professed prophetess, Jezebel, is luring early Christians away from their spiritual practice by offering them food that was previously sacrificed to idols.

Glossary of Terms

amen – is a Westernized version of *AUM*, which has long been known as a symbol of the sound of God or the sound of Life. When you become silent and go inside your mind to listen, you will hear something that sounds like a great, rushing roar, or the sound of millions of insects buzzing and chirping. This sound of moving energy is said to contain everything that exists, ever did exist, or ever could exist.

ancestors – the source of much misinformation and sin handed down from one generation to the next, and the instigators of traditions that bind culture in such a way that individual change is extremely difficult. This is why you hear the phrase, "…he is suffering from the sins of the father…"

anoint – an ancient ceremony or ritual carried out in acknowledgment that one had achieved Christ-consciousness and activated the gifts of vision, healing, wisdom, etc. Sometimes the gifts themselves are said to be the anointing.

awaken – a term used to denote a degree of awareness and knowledge of God. To "awaken" spiritually means to become aware of Love, or to be able to see at least some amount of the Light that makes up the spiritual world, or to become supremely conscious of the great knowing and power associated with God. Awakening also refers the awareness that *you are part of God* and carry that all-knowing, all-powerful Being within yourself, which is known as The Christ.

Babel – originally a reference to the story of the Tower of Babel in which man planned to build a tower high enough to reach heaven and which God supposedly ruined by causing all the humans to speak in different languages so no one could understand anyone else. Today the term "Babel" has come to mean "a confusing mix of words, talk, sounds, languages, and confusion all being heard at once, with no one really understanding anyone else."

Babylon – like the ancient city of Babylon that was destroyed, this term refers to a city, nation, or organization that is corrupt.

Bible – a collection of ancient writings by prophets, prophetesses, and seers of old.

Body of Christ – includes every man, woman, and child that has discovered and developed their inner Christ, become a Son or Daughter, and joined the community of oneness that operates in full abundance, compassion and generosity to one another, without being subject to death, disaster, or illness.

carnal mind – the ordinary workings of the human mind and mentality. Often refers to logic, reasoning, excuses, etc.

channeling – spoken prophecy, as opposed to written prophecy.

charity – an action based on love.

Christ – within each human being is the unique seed of God which contains the full potential of that individual human and is called *the Christ within*. When fully developed, that potential leads each to become a Son or Daughter of God.

Christ-consciousness – an extraordinary form of consciousness that can only be described as all-seeing (you can see through everything), all-knowing (you are on an intimate basis with every particle, molecule, and form in the world and beyond), and all-powerful (you are aware that every movement of thought or word shifts and re-creates the entire world). It is an order of consciousness beyond anything we are familiar with in our limited physical reality. This form of consciousness, with all its gifts and abilities, is possible when one has activated the Christ within.

clay – refers to the physical body or material things of the world.

closet – a term often used to convey the private, internal effort that must go into developing the Christ within and Christ-consciousness. E.g. "go into your private closet to pray and meditate on the Christ and learn His or Her ways."

Comforter – the Holy Spirit, or the Spirit of Truth that gives you wisdom, insight, and knowledge of everything, even that which is hidden.

Covenant – one or more agreements with God that teach the steps necessary to come into alignment with Him.

cross – symbolizes letting go of (dying to) your old ideas, thoughts, habits, and ways of being in order to practice the ideas, thoughts, habits, and ways of the Christ. Also symbolizes the crossroad one comes to when making the decision to develop the God-self.

crowned in the Kingdom of god – the term *crowned* means to take control of your life in such a way that you can develop your full potential as a human being, move into Christ-consciousness, and enjoy the Love, gifts, and power that this makes possible in your kingdom (your reality).

crucify – to let go of your old life.

dangerous – to those Beings who have developed the Christ and all of its powers, we humans are considered to be dangerous and undisciplined, thus all power is denied us until we have thoroughly let go of the thinking and habits of the world and moved into oneness with the will of God.

darkness – today's world is said to exist in darkness simply because we are undeveloped and do not generate the Light that a fully developed, mature human emits once the Christ has been developed.

Daughter of God – a woman who has developed the inner Christ to the point that she now begins to generate light. She has so perfectly aligned her will with God's will that she becomes a perfect expression of individual and unique life, love, health, joy, abundance, and freedom from death. She is also able to *see* the heaven-worlds made of Light and the God-Beings who exist in those dimensions of reality.

death – occurs when an individual has spent too much time focused on worldly and material issues, and not enough time focused on God – for God is *life*. Anything that is *not life* comes to an end. God is *life* and is the only thing that is eternal. Thus, only the things associated with God will last forever, things like love, joy, health, truth, unlimited abundance, etc.

deliverance – developing the Christ delivers you from the world of fear, anger, war, injustice, sickness, pain, and sorrow. Instead you receive the gifts of clarity, wisdom, power, vision, healing, and other abilities, all of which remove the many restrictions and limits imposed by physical life.

devil – supposedly a horned man with hooves for feet and a tail, however, to "devil" something is to cook it or heat it and thus the term *devil* was used to signify anything that caused "burning guilt," "burning shame," or "burning embarrassment and disappointment."

divine guidance – the excellent advice and timely direction that comes from the Christ within us any time we ask for it.

double-eyed – to follow the ways of the world and its laws, while trying to follow spiritual law and reach the high levels of consciousness that lead to Christ and the heaven-worlds.

Egypt – this term is used in a manner similar to the way *Babylon* is used – to denote a nation or group that is arrogant and cursed by sickness and corruption.

enlightenment – occurs when the Christ-self is fully activated and the individual begins to generate and radiate Light, resulting in a pronounced glow around them that can be seen with the physical eyes. This is also accompanied by great gifts of vision and wisdom.

epistle – a formal letter or written message.

eternity – we leave the world of time and step into the world of eternity when we stop basing our decisions and actions on the past or the future and instead follow the guidance, insight, and direction of the Christ who attends ONLY to the present. In the present we make a full commitment to creating joy, maintaining peace, trusting abundance, and understanding the perfection, wholeness, and truth of each moment.

evergreen – a symbol of eternal life and freedom from darkness, sickness, and death.

faith – the willingness to continue thinking and acting as if the Christ within you is there and is developing, even if there are no outward signs of that Presence yet.

flesh – a general reference to humanity or the physical world, as opposed to the literal interpretation of "skin and bones."

forgiveness – the act of overlooking the hundreds of words and acts each day that invite you to dive back into the world of fear, worry, vengeance, and judgment. The hardest part about forgiveness is that when you first begin to practice it, you often don't know what to say or how to respond when someone introduces a conversation based on anger, judgment, fear, etc.

freedom – to be free of problems, sickness, frustrations, injustices, angers, accidents, death, and other limitations of physical reality.

glory – giving glory refers to giving someone credit for doing something. This term is also used to refer to the extraordinary Light that radiates out of those Beings who have developed the Christ and activated it fully.

goats – those who stubbornly refuse to follow Spiritual Law or who choose to remain ignorant about God and the Christ.

God – is *Life*, which is eternal. Also, the combination of consonants *G* and *D*, and the vowel *O* make up the sound *God*, and these three sounds have a the power to affect and move Life into desired configurations of form and action.

Godhead – a term that is used synonymously with *God*.

Grace – think of Grace as if it were similar to water behind a dam. If you poke a little hole in the dam, the water immediately flows through it. If you remove the dam you will immediately be engulfed in the water. If you remove the blocks to love, love immediately flows into you. Grace is akin to force, the force of God that instantly and completely engulfs and flows through you when you remove the obstacles to love.

heart – symbolizes the seat of Christ-consciousness, which is characterized by an all-encompassing Love.

heaven – a very high-frequency dimension of existence inhabited by highly evolved Beings that we think of as "Gods" and where everything is made of Light rather than material substance.

hell – a term used to represent any situation, condition, or world that is not in alignment with God. These worlds are filled with anger, war, cheating, lies, verbal attack, or the fears that both create these or result from these. Hell is often referred to as the state or condition that results when you separate your mind from God's, and is any place that is *not* heaven.

higher consciousness – is characterized by a very high brain-wave frequency, which when stabilized, allows one to begin seeing the Light of which everything is made. Also refers to the ability to maintain a focus on Love and an alignment with Life.

highest consciousness – the level of consciousness maintained in the heaven worlds, often referred to as the Kingdom of the Most High.

holy – something that is considered sacred because it is part of God and part of the oneness of Life. We could say something is "whole," or perhaps "wholly one," and still understand that it is part of the oneness, but when we say it is "holy" we convey the "sacred and eternal" aspect of that thing and a willingness to honor it.

Holy Spirit – a unique form of Intelligence created by Jesus in order to teach, guide, and lead every human being to their own path of development, eventually bringing them into relationship with the Christ within.

humility – the constant awareness that you, as a human body, are powerless and fated for death until the Christ within you is activated and developed. Once that Christ has been awakened, even though there are gifts associated with that, you remain aware that it all comes from God and you are simply a channel of God, doing particular things in His name. The old you steps aside to let the God-self take over.

I Am – an ancient name given to the great, mysterious force of Life, which we usually call God.

idol – anything that you think is more important than God, or that you listen to instead of listening to the still, small voice of God within yourself.

inner teacher – the "still, small voice" of the Christ within that guides you moment-by-moment and day-by-day to do what is right in every situation, nurturing the Life you already have and extending it into eternity.

intercession – to step into a situation in order to help one another, strengthen someone, distract them from a poor attitude, pray and ask for help for them, support them, or some other kind and compassionate assistance. If we were fully developed, the help we offer would be miraculous and immediate.

Israel – an ancient term originally used to indicate those Beings who had reached eternal Life and lived in the kingdom of Light. They were also able to supersede the laws of physical reality. The word is composed of three parts. *Is* which denotes *the eternal*, *Ra* which refers to the *Light*, and *El* which is the highest form of consciousness one can maintain and still remain a physical being.

judgment – the habit of constantly deciding what is good or bad, more desirable or less desirable, rich or poor, pretty or ugly, proper or improper, tasteful or distasteful, and on and on, all of it based on the criteria you learned from the material world.

kingdom of God – in the heaven-world each soul is referred to as a kingdom. As a member of the heaven-world, the soul creates and contributes to a beautiful, healthy, loving reality that is integral to what all the other souls are creating. When you activate the Christ within yourself, you begin to build the kingdom of God in and around you, with the God-self in charge of everything you do. The collective reality created by many perfectly integrated kingdoms is called *heaven* and is often referred to as the Kingdom of God, a singular term, because oneness prevails there.

Lady – a fully developed female Christ.

Last Judgment – although this has long been taught to be a mythical point in the future when God judges all the remaining humans and takes the believers to heaven with him, the last judgment is an individual event in each life and occurs at the time one commits to developing Christ-consciousness and no longer indulges in judging others by using the standards of the material world, but instead practices great love and allows the Christ to make decisions.

Life – an eternal force made of Intelligent Light and characterized by extraordinary bliss. Life is what we refer to as *God*.

Light – the endless spectrum of Intelligent Light that contains far more light than the human eye can see. The heaven-worlds are made primarily of very high frequency light rather than material substance. Also, each speck of light contains the full consciousness of God, or the *I Am*, and is the *visual element* of the Godhead. The *feeling* of God is love – which is the force by the intent to create, and the *voice* of God is the *word* or *seed sound* that actually brings the Intelligent Light into formation as something that can be seen.

Living Light – refers to the fact that Light will feed, restore, energize, and renew us daily if we would learn to utilize it.

Lord – a fully developed male Christ.

love – the ability to blend your own mind and heart with the mind and heart of another person and to respond not only with kindness and compassion, but do so in such a way that this joy and love is triggered in the other person as well.

Mammon – the world of selfish money, riches, and wealth that helps no one.

manna – the form of Light that was used to feed and nurture the body before we began to depend on food. It is sometimes called the Bread of Life.

maturity – refers to the potential of the human being to become a living Christ.

meekness – the willingness to do as directed by the Christ within, even if it makes no sense at the time. The trust is that God, or the Christ, has a longer, deeper, broader view and knows what is needed at each moment or in each situation.

Most High – the dimension of existence characterized by the highest consciousness.

mixtures – the tendency to mix your own thoughts, ideas, concepts, beliefs, and will in with God's Law and Will, which corrupts the purity and perfection that is possible with His Will.

New Day – the day you activate the Christ in yourself.

New Jerusalem – a term used to convey the fact that your body is the temple of the Christ. When you turn to that Christ and begin to develop it, you will simultaneously heal and change both the temple of your body and the reality (the kingdom) you exist within thus creating a "New Jerusalem" or a new environment of sacredness for yourself.

New Pentecost – refers to the emergence of the Christ in today's world.

obedience – the willingness to honor and follow spiritual law and to do as one is directed by the Voice of God, which comes through the Christ within each person.

peace – often called the Peace of God, this is total freedom from stress, fear, or worry simply because you have absolute trust and faith in the far-seeing, all-knowing wisdom and power of God to handle everything and take care of you in the process.

Pentecost – the term means *fifty*, but usually refers to the emergence of the Christ in the apostles fifty days after Jesus' death and resurrection.

perfection – this term is used to denote someone who has let go of their old thoughts, ideas, words, and actions and has developed perfect alignment with God and His will.

Pharisee – a derogatory term for someone who follows the rules and regulations of a religion, church, or government yet has no real love, compassion, or caring for his fellow man. Since the entire teaching of God is that we are all one and each of us is an undeveloped God or Goddess, the various religions and institutions can sometimes miss the mark entirely.

pour out His spirit – occurs constantly because of the nature of God. It is to direct the force of love that holds each of us in form in such a way that we become conscious of the voice or spirit of Christ within and begin to change our life to be more in accordance with Spiritual Law rather than material law.

power – the ability to transcend physical laws, to heal instantly, to see and know without limit, and to create anything immediately according to your need or the demands of the situation.

prayer – to sit quietly and envision what you need, then ask God to fill that need out of His abundance and love.

Presence – sometimes used to refer to the Christ that is present in each of us.

prophecy – a gift that comes as one develops the Christ within the self and that consists of seeing visions, hearing the Voice of God, knowing with conviction, recognizing signs and symbols, receiving impressions and/or feelings, and being able to understand and share the messages contained in them.

prophet – a man who hears the Voice of God or sees visions that reflect God's will and the results of not honoring His will, then shares these messages and visions with others through speaking or writing.

prophetess – a woman who hears the Voice of God or sees visions that reflect God's will and the results of not honoring His will, then shares these messages and visions with others through speaking or writing.

purity – we are said to be *pure* when we no longer have worried, vengeful, fearful thoughts or indulge in angry behaviors designed to get even with others. Also refers to the perfect love that has no hint of anger, sorrow, or pain. This perfect, pure love fills and surrounds everyone and everything, and when we live in this kind of purity, we get perfect outcomes in our work and relationships. Perfect purity occurs when we live according to the Laws of Spirit and listen only to the directions coming from the Christ in us.

rebirth – the day you activate the Christ is considered to be the day you are reborn, this time into the world of Light and Spirit.

religion – there are many kinds of religion, but all consist of a set of beliefs, dogma, and rituals designed to teach their ideas about God.

remnant – the few stragglers (often outside mainstream religion) who truly understand the message of God and who work hard to develop the Christ and stay in constant communion with this inner teacher. Thus, when things fall apart, the remnant – who are used to taking direction from the God-self – follow the guidance coming from the great wisdom hidden inside the self and survive the calamities. They then start everything over, restoring the sacred teachings in an attempt to renew the world and build a culture that nurtures the full development of the Christ in each man, woman, and child.

renewal – activation of the Christ is a process of development in which you are committed to joy, love, and doing only what you are directed to do by the Christ. Since this involves everything in your life, it also includes what you eat and drink, how you think about yourself, and the long-term result of this practice is perfect health and a body that does not age. Thus we say, "He or she has been renewed."

repent – means to "think again" or to re-think one's life, choices, behaviors, and intentions in order to make new choices, hopefully in line with spiritual laws.

resurrection – the term has long been used to refer to the fact that Jesus rose from the dead, but it also refers to the point at which an individual human succeeds in raising his or her consciousness, in effect resurrecting the long dormant Christ within.

righteous – a combination of two words – *right* and *use* – which become *righteous* when spoken together quickly. The *right use* of our life, time, and energy is only achieved when we follow the guidance of the Christ within. Sometimes we feel we must step into a situation and "rescue" someone, or perhaps *not* step in to help. Only the Christ within knows the results of any word or actual outcome of any action to be able to make the kind of decision that says "Yes, do it," or "No, stand still and be silent."

risen – to raise your consciousness to the level of the Christ.

revelation – is comprised of the individual guidance and inner direction that comes to you when you ask for help and guidance from the Christ within you. It is always fresh, and up-to-date, as well as in alignment with the will of God.

sacrifice – refers to your willingness to let go of your life as you know it, your pride, your relationships, your career, and everything that once defined you in order to let your life be directed by God through the Christ in you. If some of these things are returned to you, then your job is to manage them with great care and the consciousness of a steward rather than an owner.

salvation – this word is terribly misunderstood and is often used in sentences like, "Jesus is our salvation," or similar form. Jesus did not save us from *our* "sins," he saved *himself* from the effects and results of the physical and material world. He did, however, try to teach us what we had to do to accomplish the same thing. *Salvation* is something each person must do for themselves. You begin by listening to your own talk and paying attention to your thoughts in order to eliminate anything that is destructive to yourself or others. The eventual result is that you stop creating difficulties and furthering your troubles, in effect "saving" yourself from the difficulties you used to jump blindly into and become enmeshed in. This brings peace of mind and leads toward Christ-consciousness.

Satan – usually thought of as the name of the devil, however, it often refers to the material world, which so easily bedevils us and our intentions.

selah – a term similar to "Amen" that simply means "yes, let it be."

selflessness – setting aside the ego and emptying yourself completely in order to focus on and develop the Christ.

separation – the state one is in when he or she is focused on the material world rather than on the heaven-world.

serpent – is the symbol of the material world and the temptation to become totally caught up in it, thus neglecting the true reality. The serpent crawls on its belly, symbolizing low, unawakened consciousness. The serpent is often called *Satan*.

sheep – those who willingly choose to align themselves with God and Life, follow the laws of the spiritual world, and develop the Christ.

silence – being free of all distracting thoughts and ideas

sin – is any thought, idea, fear, behavior, attitude, action, or expectation that is not based in love and Life. Since every idea, fear, thought, etc. creates another little piece of your reality, if you practice fearful, hateful, distrustful, selfish, disloyal, jealous, or otherwise destructive thoughts and actions, your body, mind, and life will reflect these. You will be plagued by failures, sickness, frustration, and eventually death.

Single-mindedness – a concentrated focus on the Christ within as the expression of your God-self to the point that you gradually transform yourself and let go of the physical world in order to enter the heaven worlds.

Son of God – a man who has developed the inner Christ to the point that he now begins to generate light. He has so perfectly aligned his will with God's will that he becomes a perfect expression of life, love, health, joy, and abundance. A Son experiences freedom from death and is also able to *see* the heaven-worlds made of Light and the God-Beings who exist in those dimensions of reality.

Sonship – refers to the group of men and women who have developed the Christ and reached the level of perfect alignment with God, and who are known as *Sons* and *Daughters*. This group of Beings is sometimes called the *Body of Christ*.

Source – another name for God, who is the source of all Life and all things.

Spirit – the intelligent, living Light that *is* God

spirit, a – a reference to a Being who has reached the God-self and exists in that dimension.

steward – to take responsibility for making something successful without feeling like it is yours or that you own it. Rather, you are simply taking the best care of it that you possibly can during the time it is yours to care for.

suffering – the sorrow, sickness, sadness, pain, etc. that result from our choices. Suffering teaches us to make new choices, finally leading to the decision to choose God by developing the Christ within ourselves.

sure and current words – the daily guidance that comes from the inner teacher, the Christ, which we are to follow without hesitation.

surrender – the willingness to give up your willfulness and instead be guided by the will of God.

thought-life – refers to one's collection of thoughts, concepts, and ideas and the effects and activity they generate in and around each human being.

time – a construct used in the physical world in order to create reasons and the logic we deem necessary for making decisions. Nearly all decisions are based on what we did in the past or what we want in the future.

Tree of Knowledge of Good and Evil – this tree is symbolic of the material, physical world with its endless judgment, sorrow, pain, sickness, and death. Those who are still caught up in the physical world, who believe it is real, *and* that the physical world is all that exists are said to be branches or leaves on the Tree of Knowledge of Good and Evil.

Tree of Life – this tree is symbolic of the Source of Life and the joy, health, abundance, love, and freedom from death available in the heaven worlds. Those who become perfectly aligned with the thought and will of God are said to be branches of the Tree of Life, while God is referred to as the trunk. Those who are aligned with God enjoy all His gifts and wisdom, along with eternal Life.

tribulation – the period of time immediately after you let go of your old life in order to follow the Christ within. This term also refers to the period of time in which a city or nation reaps the results of decision-making that is based on selfishness, arrogance, greed, injustice, war, lies, murder, etc. Only those things that are based in love will be self-sustaining and self-renewing. Everything else will self-destruct, causing great tribulation for those who are unprepared or ignorant.

Truth – refers to the only reality that is eternal and unchanging in its love and joy. It is sometimes used to denote what is *real,* as opposed to what is unreal, and only that which is self-sustaining and self-renewing is considered real. God – or Life – is the only truth.

Voice of God – sometimes called "the still, small voice within," the Voice of God comes from deep in your heart, reflects Truth, and will direct you flawlessly toward peace, healing, and love.

Void, The – when you enter into the full experience of God, the physical world disappears and you become a mass of intelligent, twinkling lights that know only one thing – *I Am!* In this experience you realize that you are *Life* and there is an indescribable bliss and power in the experience. Since physical reality is not visible or apparent while in the Void, nor is it wanted, needed, or even thought of, the ancients have long called it *The Void* and described it as *the place where you are empty of everything except God.*

worship – to honor and treat with respect and even reverence; to offer humble assistance while believing in the central importance of what you are honoring and assisting.

Zoe – an ancient term that means "life."

"Newsletters From Christ"

This collection of messages was received through the seeking of some for the teachings of The Holy Spirit in a sincere desire to know His mind and will.

The messages were shared in a series of newsletters published in 1996-97 and now are being more widely shared through this website:

www.thehistoryoftheoriginofallthings.com.

The nine volumes in the *Instructions From Heaven* series have been published for the benefit of all sincere seekers of truth. Through divine guidance and permission these sacred messages are being shared. It is the hope of the ones who received these messages that The Lord will be seen and revered in these words, and that others may be helped thereby. He that has an ear, let him hear what the Spirit of Truth says to him and the Church in the Earth Kingdom at this hour.

Index

A

A.W.O.L., 146
Abraham, 64
abundance, 115
Abundance, 192
abyss, the, 84
accidents, 207
Adam, 34
Adam and Eve, 127
Adam's sin, 197
adulterous people, 134
airplane, the, 63
alarm in Christendom, an, 189
alignment, complete, 159
alignment, right, 184
ancestors, 112, 213
angels, 63
anoint, 213
anointing, 18, 82
anointing oil, 197
answers, listening for His, 16
anti-Christ, 131, 164
Apostles, 75
appearance, your, 30
archaeologists, 146
arrogance, 59, 187
attitude, your, 31
attitudes, 185
AUM, 213
authority, challenge to your, 187
authority, fable of man's, 72
authority, inner, 100
awaken, 213
Awaken fully to My Presence, 180

B

Baal, 211
Babel, 214
Babylon, 120, 168, 209
Babylon, the religious harlot, 131
bad habits, 60
baggage of the world, 62
bank, 178
bank accounts, 135
bank, savings in the, 178
battle, 158, 160
be as you are, 37
Beast is the government, the, 131
Beast, the, 131
beauty, true, 39
beginning, in the, 209
Being alive in Spirit, a, 39
being the creature He made you, 30
Being, new type of, 116
Belial, 210
bible college, 92
Bible, the, 8, 92
big picture, the, 42
birth pangs, 197
blasphemer, 131
blasphemy, 187
blind, 120
blindness, 127
Blindness is rampant, 131
blue ribbon committee, 94
boasting, 70
Body of Christ, 214
Body of Christ, the, 13, 25
Body, One, 108
body/mind, 54, 58
body/mind, your, 191
bondage and captivity, 66
bondwoman, Christendom is the, 206
Book of Life, My, 166
books, 130, 145, 152
Bread of Life, 119
breath of Spirit, breathe the, 209
brothers and sisters, 63
brothers and sisters, hurting you, 31
butterfly, 116

C

calling, your, 68
captivity, release from, 170
careers, 111
carnal mind, 214
Carnal wisdom, 206
caterpillar, 63
Catholicism, 131

chains of fear, unlock your, 199
chains of your own making, 70
change, 49, 101
change on Earth, time for, 102
change your thinking, failure to, 63
change your ways, 188
change, the call to, 135
changes in you, 109
changing your worldly habits, 51
chaos, 135
chaos, coming, 52
charity, 214
child, become like a, 76
children of the street, 201
Christ, 214
Christ in yourself, the, 33
Christ Self, 47
Christ within, 69
Christ within, the, 24, 149
Christ, experience of, 65
Christ, manifesting the, 131
Christ, the, 57, 60, 165
Christ-consciousness, 8, 62, 82, 107, 152, 157, 159, 179, 214
Christendom, 49, 94, 121, 131, 189
Christendom as devised by men, 66
Christendom doomed, 89
Christendom, barren pastures of, 81
Christendom, sytems of, 50
Christendom, the nations of, 161
Christianity, 37
Christ-mind, 68, 76
Christ-state, 61
church and state, 168
Churches, 157
churches, the, 128
Circumcise your heart, 165
circumcision, 197
cities thrown down, great, 137
clay, 55, 95, 109
cleanse you of your *self*, 63
cleanse yourself, 185
cleansing, 49, 53
cleansing floods of Truth, 172
clods, hardened, 85
closet of your private self, 114
closet, private, 105
closets, 202
closets, private prayer, 171
Clothes, 39

clothing, 134, 186
cocoon, 169
commitment, 30-fold, 114
COMMUNE TOGETHER, 34
communion, constant, 194
communion, perpetual, 16
compassion, 181
computers, 63
conceit, high-minded, 185
conformity, 85
conscience, 85
conscience at rest, 71
conscience of humanity, 133
consciousness, 114, 119, 136, 147, 156
consciousness of heaven, 143
consciousness, frequencies of, 56
consciousness, higher, 83, 97, 107
Consciousness, Higher, 112
consciousness, highest, 67
consciousness, raise your, 44, 51, 85, 161
continents, 172
Correct yourself, 208
corrections for self, 100
creature of the dust, 169
cross, 51, 113
cross, My, 50
crown of everlasting life, 179
crucifixion for your judgment, 31
curse of Adam's sin, 197

D

damnation and destruction, 169
dangerous with My Power, 61
darkness, 70, 97, 106, 127, 155
darkness in your kingdom, 204
Dathan, 121, 168
death, 49, 92, 114
Death, 163, 169
death and disobedience, 127
Death is the result, 43
death of old ways, 116
death to self multiplies Life, 199
death, curse of, 208
death, emptiness, and darkness, 129
death, learning to overcome, 29
death, religion's, 69
death, repeated, 98

death, rid you of, 45
death, shadow of, 170
death, shadow of, 120
death, the ways of, 209
Death?, What is, 127
decisionmaking, 172
decision-making, faulty, 86
deliver, power to, 163
deliverance, 49
Deliverance from all fear, 199
deliverance to others, 118
deliverance, the path of, 88
denominational hands, 70
destiny, absolute, 100
destruction and damnation, 192
destruction, day of, 137
develop yourself, 88
development, stage of, 183
Devil, they will call Me, 198
dialogue with Him daily, 22
difficult times, 117
difficulties, facing, 182
diligence, 156, 180
dimensions of existence, 56
dimmer switch, 119, 204
direction, pure, 174
disbelief, state of, 188
discipline, 118
disobedience, 164
Disobedience, 133
DNA, spiritual, 126, 143
doctrine, 140
doctrine and tradition, 120
doctrine of lies, 165
doctrine, changing winds of, 130
doctrine, poisonous, 164
doctrines, 48
doctrines of emptiness, dogmatic, 167
Don Haughey, 8
double agents, 171
double-eyed, 129
double-minded, 129, 139, 192
Doubt, 161
downtrodden, uplift the, 195
dragon, the, 202
dross, your, 61
dual citizenship, 194
dust, 59, 135
duty, drudgery, and loathing, 154
dying to old self, 110

E

ears to hear, 78, 163
earth groans, 196
earth must adjust, 196
Egypt, 161, 209
electronics, 63
Elijah, 207
Emotion?, What is, 127
empty yourself, 177
emptying yourself, 58, 118
end days, 77, 172, 193
end of days, 164
enlightened, become, 194
enlightenment, 75
enlightenment, secondary, 109
Essence of Life, 47, 48, 129, 169
essence of power, 118
eternal Life, 48
Eternal Life comes from your Redeemer, 200
Eternal Life, step into, 85
evergreen, 154
everlasting love, 195
everlasting principles, 193
everlasting things, 192
evil course, pursuing an, 208
examples, you are, 60
excavators, 146
eye focus on Me, Let your, 196
eye to see, 78
eyes focused on Me, 204

F

fable, 72
fables, 140
FAITH, 162
faith as calmness, 84
false teachings, 66
fame, 121
Families, 117
family, 63
family of man, 30
famine, 172
feed my people the Truth, 172
feel Me, you know how to, 43
fellowship, 38
fellowship, love of, 206
fields, 96

fields, plowing your, 188
First Fruits, 110, 112
First Love, 69
FIRST LOVE, 120, 206
FIRST LOVE, return to your, 130
fishes and five loaves, two, 78
flesh, 43
follow my example, 29
food in hungry times, 135
foods, necessary, 119
fool, God is not a, 208
fool, You are a, 185
forefathers, 112
forgiveness, 64, 85, 144, 147
Forgiveness, 192
forgiveness, acknowledgment of, 181
forgiveness, principle of, 108
free man of himself, 63
free will, 94
free will, man's, 36
freedom, 49, 65, 77
frequencies, 56
fruit, bitter, 44
fruitful seeds, 199
full of yourselves, 59

G

Garden of Eden, 127
garden, each is a, 41
gate, the narrow, 62
gate, the straight and narrow, 208
generations, successive, 205
genocide of innocents, 205
gift, My, 75
gifts of the Christ, 10
gifts, learning to use your, 28
giving to get, 132, 141
goats, 170
God, 57, 121
God consciousness, 40, 44, 52
God nature, your, 54
God of Life and Spirit, 83
God of the past, 119
God within, 55
God, the place of, 135
God's will, 56
God's words give life, 21
gods, 56
gods of earth, 180, 210

gods, convenient, 211
God-self, 24
gold, 186
gold, refined, 125
Gospel of Peace shoes, 158
gospel songs, 130
gospels, bitter, 85
government of men, 131
government, Heaven's, 194
governmental consent, 79
governments, 94, 168, 172
governments, new, 173
grace, 81
graduate seminars, 167
gratitude and respect, 15
green pastures, 46
grow up in Me, 158, 165
growth, 139
growth in Him, 203
Growth is determined by, 192
growth, rate of, 35
growth, stage of, 76
guidance, 184

H

habits, 115
hail, 136
hair, 72
harlot, exposing the, 189
harps, 120
hate, 203
haughty, the, 136
heal, power to, 118
healing, 166
healing Light, 197
healing Power, 116
healing that never happens, 85
health, 179
heart as a territory, 71
heart as center of joy, 110
heart is the THRONE of Christ, 110
heart, hard, 101
heart, offering your, 178
heart, reading the, 185
heart, sincerity of, 99
heart, throne of your, 195
heart-rooms, 204
heathen, 86
heaven, 109, 129

Heaven, 192
heaven is within you, 36
heaven world, 111
heaven worlds, 23, 37, 56, 83, 89
heaven worlds, brothers and sisters in the, 112
hell, 129
hidden, nothing is, 195
higher consciousness, 108
Higher Consciousness, 169
higher view, 125
highest consciousness, 110
holy, 54
HOLY LOVE AFFAIR, 110
Holy Scriptures, 35
Holy Spirit guidance, 93
Holy Spirit's direction, 146
Holy Spirit's instruction, 188
horse of doubt, 161
house of cards, 162
House, a new, 78
house, saving your, 200
houses, 111
human nature, 195
humanity, stains of your, 188
humble attitude, 158
humble heart, 37
humility, 45, 54, 59, 118, 181
hurricanes, 136
husband, a faithful, 134
husbandman, 123, 124
husks, 157
husks of man, 170
husks of men, 76

I

I Am, 57, 58, 76, 101, 105, 114, 149
I Am is a Living God, 168
I Am of old, 105
I Am says to you, the, 102
I Am the Grace, 38
I AM THE I AM, 210
I Am your mirror, 108
I Am, praise for the, 192
I Am, the, 83, 182, 189, 195
I Am, the power of the, 34
I Am, worship the, 115
I come to each of you, 165
idolatry, 103, 111

IDOLATRY BEFORE GOD, 12
idols, 69, 111, 172
idols and flexibility, 99
idols of money and gold, 210
idols, do not cling to, 196
ignorance, 179
ignorance, your, 209
Immortal Bread of Life, 81
impatience, 84
impressions, mental, 14
Infinite Wisdom, 92
inner change, 128
inner closet, your, 209
inner life, 193
inner peace, 42
inner powers, 193
inner principle, 47
inner self, Truth of your, 190
inner spiritual condition, 179
inner stillness, 145
Inner Teacher, 66
Inner Teacher, your, 24, 209
inner voice, your, 46
inner wars, 133
innocent victims, 103
insects buzzing, 213
institutions, 172
intention, your, 179
intercession, 158, 159
interdependence, 182
Ishmael, 87
Israel, 65, 80, 113, 207
ISRAEL, 101

J

Jesus, 73, 86, 209
Jesus Christ, 81
JESUS CHRIST, 129
Jesus the Christ, 132
Jezebel, 130, 134
Jezebel, Spirit of, 210
jigsaw puzzle, Creation as, 65
John the evangelist, 187
journey to the Light, 183
joy, Through, 194
Judas, 40, 171
Judging bodies, 40
judging character, 183
judgment, 60, 61, 185

judgment and its punishment, 97
justice, lower forms of, 133

K

Key of Life, 165
Key of Love, 199
king's palaces, 187
Kingdom, 146
kingdom built in you first, My, 36
kingdom of darkness and dust, 195
kingdom of flesh, 49
Kingdom of Heaven, citizens of the, 194
Kingdom of Love, 195
kingdom of the dust, 194
Kingdom, entering My Eternal, 76
kingdom, individual, 111
Kingdom, obtaining the, 70
kingdom, you are an individual, 110
kingdoms, each of your, 204
kings, rulers, and popes, 194
knowledge, adult, 75
knowledge, laying aside prior, 88
Korah, 121

L

laboring, stop your, 116
Lady within, 57
land is recreated, 137
Law of Moses, 86
law of the eternal kingdom, 76
law, letter of the, 35
laws of Heaven, 194
laws of men, 86
laws, inner, 61
laws, little book of, 91
laws, no Life in your, 35
laws, rule of Spiritual, 36
learning delayed, 191
learning vs. Truth, 163
leaven, 152
leaven added to messages, 19
lessons, life, 152
letting go, 72, 100, 111
letting go of ignorance, 37
letting go of self, 49
Liberation, 158
Life, 114, 127, 163

life and health, 179
Life come from, Where does, 200
Life Eternal, Himself, 92
Life Eternal, laying hold of, 118
Life within you, strengthen, 197
life, Choose, 205
Life, Choose, 208
Life, flow of, 117
Life, restoring, 114
Life, resurrection of, 75
Life?, What is, 127
lifestyle changes, 178
Light of My consciousness, 170
Light of Truth, the, 35
Light within, the, 194
Light, developing the, 165
listening for the Voice of Spirit, 36
live forever, 127
living Christ, 47, 126
Living Epistles, 144, 167
Living God, 140, 145, 182
living sacrifice, 180
Living Water, 47, 111
LIVING WATER, 55
log in your own eye, 61, 185
Lord within, 57
Lord within is the only God, the, 136
Love, 192
LOVE AFFAIR, our, 42
love one another, 25
LOVE ONLY GOD, 208
Love, take a stand for, 158
Love, unconditional, 203
Love's grandest chord, 89
low life, 88
low self, 110

M

Mammon, 121
man's will, 92
man's wisdom, 130
manna, 48
Martin Luther, 87
mask of happiness, 155
masks of fear, 71
masters, two, 76
mature, 162
maturity, 106, 139, 145, 148, 174
maturity and growth, 191

maturity as a Christ, 37
maturity quickly, come to, 195
maturity, bring forth our, 185
meek, Blessed are the, 138
MEEK, the, 59
Mercy, 192
millstone around your necks, 167
mind quiet, 110
mind, taking charge of your, 33
miracles, 83, 166
mirror of My Truth, 32
misinformation, 213
missionaries, 166
mistakes, 151, 183
mistakes, judgment of, 203
Mixtures, 192
mixtures, writing without, 17
money, 111, 129
money as savior, 137
morality, 49
morality laws, useless, 35
mortality, 141
Moses, 113, 207
murder, 187
My Ark, 54
My authority, 64
My Authority, 186
My Body, 53
My Cleansing Fire, 64, 71
My cleansing fire of Truth, 190
My Comforter, 65, 66, 114
My Coming is different for all, 197
My criteria for judgment, 31
My Cross, 145
My fires, 188
My fullness, 158
My Gospel, 202
My grace, cut off from, 189
My Guidance, submitting to, 188
My Holy Spirit instruction, 179
My Holy Substance, 129
My Kingdom, 181
My Kingdom, entry into, 61
My Kingdom, to enter, 185
My Love, express, 188
My Nation, 81
My pattern, 166
My Promise, 85, 192
My Purpose, 196
My radiance, 57

My reign, 193
My Resurrection, 75
My Revelation, 75
My righteousness, 194
My Saints, 204
My Sons and Daughters, becoming, 175
My training, 54
My True Church, 139
My Voice, 115
My Will, follow, 112
My Word heals you, 44
My words are your Bread, 45
myth, 72, 140
myths and fables, 172

N

nations, 116
nations, blindness of, 197
natural disasters, 16
natural events, 207
nature, forces of, 103
nature, man's restrictive, 203
nature, signs in, 14
nature's fury, 137
new birth experience, 128
New Day, 105, 170
NEW DAY, 120
new day comes, 173
New Earth, 157, 168
new in old bottles, 93
New Jerusalem, 80
New Jerusalem Church, 87, 110
newsletters, 89
Nimrod, 136
Noah, 188
nourishment for the soul, 76
numbers or votes, 207
nutrients, 96
nutrients, life-giving, 47
nutrition, 45

O

oak tree, 153
obedience, 71, 89, 118, 178, 179, 206
obedience, blind, 206
obedient, 156
obedient one, *One,* 116

obey, 112
old habits of mind, 71
old self, 113, 182
old self cast away, 107
old self to die, allowing your, 180
old self, your, 58
old ways, 54, 58, 77
old ways, divorce yourself from, 88
old ways, dying to your, 63
old ways, habits, and beliefs, 157
oneness, 191
Oneness, essence of, 35
open and silent, persevere in being, 34
original transgression, 188
ostentation, 78
other side, the, 180, 190
outer facade, 193
outward actions, 185
overdo, do not, 179

P

paganism, 94
pain, scars of, 41
Paradise, 128
parent, 96
parent's understanding, his, 193
Parents, 117
past, paying attention to the, 201
past, the, 83
pastures, green, 209
path, the, 120
path, time to decide your, 189
patience, smallness teaches, 181
Pattern of Christ, 203
Pattern of meekness, 209
pattern of pride, 100
Pattern of the Living Christ, 126
Pattern of the Redeemer, 145
pattern, My, 107
Pattern, the Lord is your, 132
Paul, 144, 166, 167
Pay attention, 38
peace, 71, 135
Peace, 146
peace in silence, 43
peace of God, 133
peace of mind to the depressed, 195
peacemakers, Blessed are the, 138, 190

Pentecost, 66, 75, 82, 105
Pentecost, new, 106, 168
perdition, sons of, 165
perfect purity, 173
perfection of the heart, 183
perfection, attaining, 181
perfection, preparation for, 70
perfection, state of, 88
Peter, 40, 49, 62
Peter walks on water, 174
Pharaoh, 137
Pharisees, 49, 92, 153, 166, 187
picture, the bigger, 82
pilgrims and strangers, 194
pitfalls, individual, 183
plans for tomorrow, 58
poor in spirit, Blessed be the, 138
poor, the, 136
popes are temporal, 194
position and power, desire for, 210
potential, 41
potential for creation, 34
potential fullness, 193
potential, inner, 116
potentials of Life, 199
Potter, The, 95
pour out His Spirit, 23
power, 111, 118
power, manifested, 166
power, where is your, 166
powers, inner, 193
pray together, 117
prayer, 158
prayer, heart-felt, 69
prayer, length of, 99
prejudice, 76
presence, practice His, 16
PRESENT, the, 201
prestige, 121
pride, 59
principles, everlasting, 193
principles, heavenly, 192
prison, 131
prison doors, 165
private closet, 190
private prayer closet, 189
prodigal ways, 120
profit, 121, 128, 180
proof, 165
prophecies, 55

prophecy, 88, 145, 156
prophecy, spirit of, 91, 130
prophecy, spoken, 21
prophecy, the gift of, 13
prophetesses, 15
prophets, blood of true, 211
Psalm, 135
punishment, the demand for, 178
PURE IN HEART, 59
pure in heart, Blessed be the, 138
pure words, 17
purge of what is false, 202
purging, 53
purity, 178
PURITY, 107, 150
purpose for which He created you, 206
purpose, man's, 91
puzzle pieces, 163

Q

quiet inside, being, 24
Quiet yourselves, 205

R

races, all, 86
radiance, 115
REAL SUBSTANCE, 196
REAL, something, 52
Real, starving for something, 169
reason and doubt, 76
reasoning process, 19
rebirth, 154, 169, 190
rebirth in Life, 169
rebirth, season of, 108
red man, 72
redemption, the voice of, 46
regenerate you, 158
relief from stress, 199
religion, system of, 94
religion's purpose, 69
religions, worldly, 87
religious attendance, 72
remnant, 77, 136, 168, 173, 188
renewal, 190
repent, 15
repentance, 120
repentance, true, 69
reputation, your, 177

resistance, 56
responsibility, your, 68
responsible for our brothers, 25
restoration of unity, 165
resurrect you, 115
resurrected house, your, 200
resurrection, 190
Resurrection, 77
resurrection of your soul, 105
re-think your life, 100, 113
Rethink your life, 15
re-think your position, 185
retraining, 182
REVELATION, 94
revelation of one's purpose, 91
revelations, 162
revenge, 147
revenge, supposed, 179
rich, the, 135
riches, 85
right to choose, the, 157
right use, 178
Right Use of all things, 158
right use of consciousness, 112
righteous, 147
righteous, the, 135
righteousness, the world's, 62
righteousness, true, 186
rights, supposed, 133
rights, your, 178
right-use-ness, 116
rigidity, 85
River of Love, 201
ROCK, SOLID, 139
ROOT of all trouble, 94

S

sacrifice, 59
sacrifice your whole life, 71
Saints, 63, 67, 135
salvation, 109
salvation experiences, 28
salvation of yourself, 88
salvation, My intended, 193
sand, 157
sandy foundations, 130, 172
Sarkieus, 157
Satan, 40, 81, 110, 128, 135, 161, 198
Satan's bride, 211

savages, 86
saving others, 69
scorn, 146
scriptures, 140
scrolls and writings, 146
secret place of the Most High, the, 209
sect, creating a new, 27
seed in a jar, 116
seed of ancestors, 112
seed of Christ, 112
seed, their, 136
Seeds, 96
self "to death, 34
self as sinful, 67
self, control your, 33
Self, deepest, 106
self, low, 105
Self, open to your deepest, 43
self, purified from, 67
Self, true, 133
Self, voice of our deepest, 14
self-development, 9
self-examination, 71, 179, 195
self-importance, 49
selflessness, 177
self-man, your, 178
self-righteous, 184
self-satisfaction, 100
self-will, 94, 146
self-will and peace, 133
seminaries, 166, 209
sermons, 55
serpent, 113
serpent of darkness, 205
serpent, real, 46
seven things Yahweh abhors, 54
shame or guilt, 203
sheep, 66, 81, 121, 170
sheep, imprisoning, 198
shepherds, 157
sickness, 92
silence, 48, 58
silence all thoughts, 27
silence and stillness, 28
silence and stillness of your heart. *See*
silence, wait in, 33
silent and prostrate, remain, 189
silent within, be, 27
sin, 51, 92
sin, what is, 67

SINGLE-MINDEDNESS, 33
sins, 112
sins of the fathers, 136
sins press Me, your, 196
sins, unconfessed, 179
slaves to the world, 32
sleep, 16
SLEEP OF DEATH, 52
sleep, enough, 33
slothful, 191
small talk, 27
snow, 136
Sodom and Gomorrah, 136, 168
soil, 95, 123, 153
solitude, 34
Son, 150
S*on of God*, 91
Son of God, status as a, 189
Son or Daughter, 58
Son or Daughter sets you free, 32
songs, 89
Sonrise, 142
Sons and Daughters, 55, 87, 106, 148
sons and daughters of men, 55
Sons and Daughters, manifesting as, 182
Sons and Daughters, power in My, 194
Sons of God, 145, 149
*Son*shine, 41, 143
Sonship, 59, 64
SONSHIP, 88
Sonship delayed, 191
souls, 200
souls, parched and thirsty, 98
Source of Power, True, 167
SOURCE, DIVINE, 98
Source, the, 153
space walks, 63
speak in tongues, 144
spirit dialogue, 48
Spirit is an avenue, 194
spirit of your own self, 61
Spirit, learn the way of, 50
Spirit, opening to, 197
Spiritual decline, 127
splinter from your brother's eye, 61
splinter in your brother's eye, 185
statistics, 28
statues, 111

status, 111
status as a Son of God, 189
steward, 78
stewardship, 190
still small voice, a, 14
strength to overcome, 181
stress, relief from all, 199
strongholds, tearing down, 190
studies, earthly, 76
success, the mark of, 29
suicide, 159
superstition, 72, 140
surrender, 62, 180
Surrender yourself, 93
surrender, degrees of, 113
Sword of prophecy, The, 158
symbolism, 119

T

talent, 152
talents, five, 22
talents, use your, 198
tapes, 130, 145, 152
tares, 121
task force, 94
Teacher, 53, 55, 65, 76, 151, 181
teacher, substitute, 156
Teacher, your, 88
teachers, 120, 209
teachers, counterfeit, 206
teachings for you – *just you*, 35
teachings of man, 208
teachings of men, 170
teachings, sanitized, 128
teenagers, 65
Temples, 157
testing, 115
tests, 113
the Beast, 103, 132, 147, 187, 189
the Christ, 116, 120, 142, 149, 162
The Potter, 64
theological training, 166
thirsty sponges, your are dry, 198
Thomas, doubting, 207
thought is rooted in SELF, 94
thought-life, 63, 71
thoughts as weeds, 155
thoughts, prejudiced, 30
thoughts, unloving, 185

thoughts, words, or actions, 178
throne of your heart, 195
tidal waves, 136
tithes, 128
tithing, 72
tombs, 85
tombs of dead thinking, 114
tombs of your houses, 115
tornadoes, 136
tradition, imprisoned by, 199
traditions of the world, 115
traditions that bind, 213
traditions, humanity's, 48
train to Paradise, 128
transfiguration, mount of, 207
transform the past, 170
transformation, 116, 166
transgressing the Love, 190
Tree of Knowledge, 127, 163, 165, 169
Tree of Life, 127, 164, 165, 169
TREE OF LIFE, 47
trespass, 144
trespasses, 98
trials and tribulations, 60
tribulation, 177
TRUE PARENT, your, 46
trumpets, Sound the, 161
Truth of all the ages, 45
Truth, not understanding, 188
Truth?, What is, 127

U

understanding, forests of, 174
unforgiving heart, 64
unlearning Christendom, 206
unrighteous judgments, 187

V

valley of joy, 124
vanity, 186
veil of blindness, 196
veil of darkness, 206
veil, a, 164
veil, the, 54
veiled sight, 127
vessel, 95, 149
vessels fit for destruction, 188

victims, innocent, 103
VINE OF ETERNAL LIFE, 43
vineyard, 123
vision, 68, 126
Vision, 93
vision, higher, 83
Voice of My Instruction, 206
Voice of My Spirit, 174
voice, hearing the Lord's voice, 13
Void, the great, 34

W

walk, 143
walk, daily, 143
war chest, 136
war, private, 146
Water of Life, 198
waters, still, 209
weeds, 155
weight, judging someone's, 186
Wellspring of Life, 111
wholeness, 178
whore, spirit of the, 130
whoredom, spirit of, 134, 188
will of God, 133
will of Spirit, 36
will of the Father, 157
will of the flesh, 36
will, your, 57, 69, 159
willful man, 133
willful man cannot hear, 133
willingness to learn, 56

wind, the, 105
Winged Life, 77
wings, shadow of My, 42
wisdom, 173
wisdom of My Holy Spirit, 202
wolves, 121, 156
wolves in sheep's religious clothing, 129
woman's intrigue, 134
women's servitude, 72
words, 152
words, fresh and current, 191
words, new, 128
words, sure and current, 48, 66
world of darkness, Your, 190
world, blindness of your, 35
world, destruction of the, 94
worldly habits, 54
worldly self, 133
worldly wisdom, 181
worms, 169
worship, 15
writing the words of the Father, 14

Y

Yahweh, 54

Z

Zoe Babel, 14